What Is HUMAN RIGHT?

A Conceptual Guide for
Beginners, Practitioners and Policy Makers

RAJ DOCTOR

Raj Doctor is trained as an architect, town-planner and management expert. He has worked with several international not-for-profit organizations. He has travelled to more than 39 countries globally. Currently he lives in India.

Also by
Raj Doctor

Melancholy of Innocence, *Romantic Novel*
Ashtavakra – Dialogues with King Janak – *Spiritual Discourse*
Potpourri of AMOUR – Melange – *Anthology of LOVE Quotes*
Smorgasbord of Eros – *Book of Poems*
Panoply of Ode – *Book of Poems*
What Is Human Right? – *Theoretical Critique*

ISBN-13: 978-1542796439
ISBN-10: 1542796431
This book has been assigned a CreateSpace ISBN

Printed and bound at CreateSpace

Authored and Edited by: Raj Doctor

Font Garamond 8, 11, 14, 22
Normal, *Italics* and **Bold**

DEDICATED TO

The

Silent

Sufferers

Of

Human

Right

Abuses

Contents

1. *Whom Is This Book For?*

*I*t is assumed that people who work for human rights are sensitive human beings. People who are interested to know about human rights are also sensible enough to take personal interest to understand *"What is Human Right?"*

For those who are skeptics this book tries its best to appeal their humaneness by tickling their gray cells to new frontiers of understanding human rights concepts.

This last group of skeptics are expected to remain open for new ideas, because as much the book tries to explain Human Rights, it also takes liberty to look beyond the United Nations Human Rights Declaration (UNHRD) and see how relevant is UNHRD in today's times, what are its loopholes, short-comings, misplaced assumptions and biases that fails to deliver justice in real world.

Thus this book is really meant for those who are rational to understand (*even criticize*) and to further, take an objective look at the existing human rights clauses and for those who are also sensitive to the abuses and violations human being faces.

This book is for those who are aware of the limitations of the world we live in.

Surely this book does not address those who have closed their mind on looking beyond the original text of UNHRD.

This book also does not appeal to those who think that **I know everything** and have already found answers of saving the humanity, our planet and the world with 5-point or 10-way or 15- sustainable methodologies.

This book is for those who are still open and free to their own limitations of mind. This book is for those who have still some warmth remaining in their heart and tenderness in their outlook towards our beautiful planet earth.

This book is for those who are not aggressive and assertively protesting every time to drive Human Rights mandate just because it is something that is written in UNHRD and something that one considers as words engraved in stone.

This book is for those who are *FREE* to learn. This book is for those who are liberated thinkers.

Those who are stubborn and face the inability to be aware and free themselves of their own dogmas, principles and prejudices are advised to skip this book.

2. *Just an Introduction*

I am starting with a bi-tangent story to touch the sensitivity of all those who are working in social and development sector to bring up a philosophical issue related to the work one does with poor and poverty.

The same rationalization and introspection can be extended to human rights.

*W*hen one enters a poverty struck area, locality, region and/or country, one searches for recipients who are ready for their *"acceptance of poverty"* as defined by those experts, academicians, policy makers, leaders who defined poverty in their own ways and methods.

We are not talking here of disaster struck areas and regions - struck by famines, drought, floods, tsunami. The set up we are presenting here is a poor, under-developed or developing country or region.

*W*e entered a new slum to start a project on 'Removing Poverty' and 'Empowering Poor'. We walked around to see a receptive face – a recipient, who will accept us to make them realize they are poor, and they require help. *We are here to help* is the message we carried on our humble slightly smiling faces.

We roamed around each and every lane and found no acceptance. We personally know these people are "poor" but how come, they who are poor do not know they are poor?

May be, first we need to teach them and make them aware of the poverty to get our acceptance and to consider us as someone who has come to help them - a giver of something that will remove their poverty. We have money, extra money we mobilized to spend, and we have to spend them on poor and poverty. If there are no poor, we have to invent poverty by teaching them, training them, building their capacities to we can generate more money for poor by show-casing poor, poverty and our success story. (**Military Budget Analogy** – *We have budget, we will create war, if there is no war. It gives us work and keeps us busy.*)

We start by saying "We are here to do some good-work for those who need support – in terms of education, child-care, health, nutrition, hygiene, skill-building, self-help groups so on and so forth".

For sure, we did not go and make a mistake of telling them directly that they are "poor" and we have come to help poor. *Why?*

Calling someone poor in front of them on their face is snatching the human dignity with which they are living their daily lives with lots of struggle and over-coming each difficulty of life to meet their ends to survive in this harsh world.

Calling them *"poor"* is not a good start to begin our conversation and project work. It makes the whole thing look like a lot top-down approach and looking down on people who are considered poor. Very insensitive…!

Similarly, imagine entering an indigenous tribal population and seeing them naked, un-educated and calling them savages would not help either.

That was the criminal mistake early sixteenth, seventeenth and eighteenth century *explorers* committed. There was no sensitivity around approaching another human being with tenderness and love. Those who went for exploration and found un-touched human population by their definition of European development were considered and treated as something below their standards and looked down with disgust. Even missionaries where sent to reform the aboriginals with further purpose of disguised in religious expansionist ideologies.

That was the starting point of perpetuating the dominance role of the GIVER, the Philanthropist and the Missionary - who wore the false garb of savior under religious righteousness, with a posture of *"I'm better than YOU"* and *"I know how to make you like me"*

They killed the diversified and unique local traditions, beliefs and culture, and looked down on their Gods and Ghosts to make them subject to believe in have a monolithic religious (right / wrong?) undertaking of LORD.

That was the starting point of recently recognized account in history human rights abuse of another human being.

A total failed and disastrous approach to begin any contact with another unknown human being or a stranger!

*S*adly we, who go searching for poor to help them know that **we** are not "poor"; we have wealth, money, education, other comforts of life they have not ever seen. We show we are well-off than others, so we can go around with a purpose to help the poor, calling human beings – "*poor*".

In earlier times, there were fights, wars and resistance to accept invasion of foreigners with a yard-stick of I know better than you. With the might of gun-powder most of the rebellions were quelled – aboriginals killed, surrendered, abolished in a genocidal crime and later missionaries were sent to reform aboriginals to become like "*so called human beings*" – the exterminators, the killers, and the abusers.

In today's times things have changed. People in those regions and areas, the so called "*poor*" are smart enough to perceive our intentions and recognize the need for someone who has come and help them; may be give them something FREE, or at least open up some avenue to come out of their wriggle of hunger and hard conditions of life; may be the hope is that they will receive some support from individuals or organization who might have mechanisms to support people who want to work hard.

That is the hope. That is the servitude to the idea of *"poverty"*. That is a significant psychological paradigm shift by gulping their own human dignity and extending their hand for asking support and help.

This tangent example of *poverty* is just the beginning to the journey that may progress to awareness of *rights* for someone who wants to bring human dignity back to every individual.

The author hopes that the reader is able to establish the link between poverty, rights and human dignity clearly.

Actually the person who starts to work on human rights, or is interested to work in this field of human rights might be seeking to reclaim her/his rights in this purpose to help poor or help people whose rights s/he thinks are violated or not enjoyed fully.

But there are numerous people who are smart and shrewd to exploit the terrain of poor, poverty, human rights to seek benefits of wealth and power within this framework of supporting and helping the poor without a little care to reclaim their inner peace through self-introspection and awareness.

Sadly most people working for poor, poverty and/or human rights are getting paid thousand times higher remuneration than the poor for whom they work.

Those getting paid much higher and holding top post in the poverty work and human rights organizations are so called *"hypocrites"* who perpetuate the offensive and abuse of exploiting the poor, poverty and human rights framework for their own individual gain to boost their ego, gain wealth and power.

The purpose of this book is just to open up the reader's mind in a way we think differently and courageously - we expect the ray of light of openness of minds when one reads this book.

3. Human Rights in Simple Terms

The original text of United Nations Human Rights Declaration (UNHRD) is included for your reference at the end of this book.

Before we go into discussing the fundamentals and concepts used in human rights, let us understand briefly what human rights means in simple terms.

Human Rights are meant to maintain dignity of human being, so that humans can have proper personal development.

Broadly, human activities fall into these six categories: civic, political, social, cultural, religious and economic.

Thus in every aspect of our life and in any field we work, human rights are applicable.

4. Purpose and Principles of UNHRD

*I*n a straight forward way we can explain the purpose and principles of UNHRD as follows:

1. Every human has equal rights
2. People have right of self-determination
3. No nation will use threat or force on another nation. It is prohibited
4. Every nation has obligation to assist United Nations (UN)
5. No nation will assist those states that are against UN
6. Even though some nations are not members of UN, but UN will ensure that they somewhat comply to UN Principles
7. UN will not interfere in domestic matters of any nation state or country

When we discuss these concepts in details we will dissect each and every aspects of it to bring clarity in pros and cons and those important issues missed out in purpose and principles of UNHRD.

5. *Essence of* UNHRD

There are **thirty declarations** in UNHRD. The most simplified of the essence of 30 principles of UNHRD is given below:

1. We Are All Born Free and Equal

2. Don't Discriminate

3. The Right to Life

4. No Slavery

5. No Torture

6. You Have Rights No Matter Where You Go

7. We're All Equal Before the Law

8. Your Human Rights Are Protected by Law

9. No Unfair Detainment

10. The Right to Trial

11. We're Always Innocent Till Proven Guilty

12. The Right to Privacy

13. Freedom to Move

14. The Right to Seek a Safe Place to Live

15. Right to a Nationality

16. Marriage and Family

6. What Are "Rights"?

Rights in its absolute sense is "doing what is right"

Doing what is 'right' means doing something that is easily understood by **majority of population perceive** as what is right and what is wrong.

If we go one step further, if suffering is a basic criterion to identify whether human rights of a person is violated or abused, one needs to define suffering.

One has to use reason, intellect and logic to define a reasonable level of suffering to say – beyond this point or level – more suffering is not permissible and someone's rights are violated after that.

Who defines the level of sufferings?

The crucial question we ask here is: Those who do not have the same aptitude to understand this *concept of rights*, why someone else should define *rights* for them and impose on them?

Who are we to define and decide the level of sufferings of anyone who cannot understand suffering in the way UNHRD drafting committee express their threshold levels of sufferings? And why should we humans be the custodians of anyone?

7. Many Unanswered Questions

*W*hy we humans, and especially in the *rights* framework a group of intellectual humans should sit together and decide a charter or rights for the whole universe and say – this is how we define rights for the whole world?

Why should representatives of states and nations ratify and sign on behalf of the whole populace the definition of *rights* and its implication on their own constituencies?

The ratification at international level is done through an official signatory of each nation state, but within a state the implementation is dictatorial and top down, because no one has taken the signature of the masses to decide "what is *right*?"

So why this top down approach in definition the *rights* and pushing it on the world?

Rights are just another form of morals.

Morals arise from individuals who feel that certain attitudes or behavior of human being is moral and certain attitudes are immoral. These individuals who hold morals of the society or a group hold truth in terms of individual agreement of right and wrong.

But we should understand that what is morally right for an individual cannot be morally right for another person or a group or for a society or for a nation as a whole.

Who defines morals and why the masses believe in those values of morals that are laid down by an individual or a group of individuals?

At what point in time do these morals become principles for society and then they take the form of legislation in a governing state?

Who pushes for these morals and why they become legislation?

When morals - in this case *rights* becomes legislations – why it is thrust down from a central authority to a federal structure of states?

Why people accept such moral principles in form of legislation and laws without realizing its evolution and its impact on a historically evolutionary culture at a particular point in time – which is different for different regions and state.

This section leaves one with a sense of gaining conceptual clarity with questions that are imminent to answer when understanding *"What are rights?"*

Through the course of these intellectual dwelling we will try to answer some of the relevant questions raised in this section.

8. How Rights Are Violated?

Violation happens through a series of events - that leads to a source of power subjugating (bringing under control) the one who is less powerful.

This is a very important definition to keep in mind when reading the entire text.

Rights violation flow through a hierarchy - hierarchy is mostly built by the amount of power restored on an individual or a group to decide on something – mostly in terms of monetary benefit to them either in "pricing" and/ or wealth of one's subjects.

In a nation, either: The King, Dictator, The Chosen One, A President or Prime Minister holds the power, though they may or may not be the richest person earning highest pay in their country, but they hold the power over budgets and course of events through wealth creation and money flow that make them powerful.

In an organization, the Head of an organization – Executive Director, Secretary General, Chief Executive Officer (CEO) and Chairperson - holds the same power, within the organization in decision making over many issues and things that govern the company and / or organization or private/ public entity.

In the case of societal structures, a community head – a village head, a wealthy land lord or business person, holds power of decision making because of direct or indirect influence over resources mainly governed by pricing and wealth in that particular society or community.

Lastly in case of a family, the person who holds the key to monetary decision making and earnings most holds the power of decision making over resource allocation and deciding the fate of family members.

Most rights violations takes place within the above mentioned scenario and premise (but not restricted only to these)

Basically, violation of rights of others always starts within a hierarchy where people – individual or group of people - hold power position to decide things for others.

To see that rights of any human being are not violated – one needs to dissolve the hierarchy structure that bestows power on individuals, a group, a committee to decide on others members.

One can only talk of protecting rights of individual from a sphere that is outside the orbit of individuals or group holding any power over single or multiple entities. If a person or group holds those positions of power – invariably they cannot claim any authority of talking about rights of others, because in the existing framework, they themselves are placed in the center of being a violators and exploiters and abuser of *rights*.

9. Short History of UNHRD

*T*hroughout the history the *"rights"* perspective was always seen as being part of a group's membership. As for example, if one is part or member of a state, an entity, a religious body, a nation – the group will provide you with certain rights for being its member.

Those rights were woven into traditions in various cultures through their religious traditions.

The precursor to **Rights bills** has various forms in history where rights were drafted for a particular section that was privileged to be granted certain rights.

*T*he declaration of human rights - UNHRD was a result arising out of two World Wars (1914 and 1944) in the span of 30 years that devastated many nations. Jewish holocaust and the nuclear bombing of Hiroshima and Nagasaki made the process of forming a UNHRD gathered more pace.

At the end of World War Two (WWII), four major world powers – three of Allied forces that joined hands to defeat Germany: USA, UK, France and one from outside the western block of continents – China, met in United States to see that there are better ways to handle world crisis than going into wars. So they made a common platform which resulted in formation of United Nations (UN) and its charter on Human Rights - UNHRD.

It was felt that UNHRD was an idea whose time was ripe and came at the juncture in history (World War II) to prevent future wars and protect individuals who may be subjected to any abuse or violations resulting out of the reasons of war.

10. An Extraordinary Vision?

The historical juncture of the events (end of World War II) made most nations to quickly agree to the proposal of emerging world order and also agree to the structure of UN and contents of UNHRD for maintaining world peace.

The process of drafting was extensive and debates were comparatively minimal, limited to nation member states of UN that raised a few points here and there; though the drafting committee would call it exhaustive in nature.

The main limitation and drawback was that the drafting committee was a male driven group – except headed by a lady (Lady Eleanor Roosevelt - the former widow of a United States President) who did not take any active role in drafting the UNHRD. The committee was mainly constituted of western educated philosophers, lawyers and jurists, diplomats and one unionist – who were studied and practiced with western perspective and outlook.

If one reads through the UNHRD clauses one would know that most wordings are ambiguous and lofty without understanding the basic reality of life and its life-forms that live in plurality in different parts of the world and without understanding that human beings are in continuous process of evolution.

Yet, the whole world was colored with one single stroke and till date the world is struggling to comply with UNHRD – a declaration which was drafted very poorly in the first place.

Though there are claims that representatives of smaller countries from Africa contributed to UNHRD, but largely no central or eastern culture and tradition were taken into account on existing historic and evolutionary timeline for drafting UNHRD.

UNHRD failed to see the complex and varied culture, tradition of various countries, religions and practices that was already existing and deeply rooted in most societies.

This in itself shows the pressure of completing the task of UNHRD within a time line and a certain level of high-handedness in which a group of individuals took upon themselves the responsibility of *power in a emerging hierarchy (ref.* as we discussed earlier, kindly remember – *power and hierarchy are debasing structures working against human rights)*

UNHRD is more of a forced doctrine of principles imposed through ratification of local nation states. Till date UNHRD is not understood by many people living in rural country side who continues to live under influence of their own society, culture and traditions from centuries. May be many have not even heard about UNHRD.

Most countries that had rich history of their own traditions are the ones that are unfortunately poor and they are the ones who cannot comply with the Western viewpoint of looking at individuals as a single entity with rights.

One can clearly read UNHRD and realize that the intent might have been good, but the process, means and assumptions are faulty.

What started with a so called noble intention become a work resembling missionaries to civilize the world as quickly as possible with the 30 Articles of UNHRD equivocal to the *Ten Commandments of Bible*.

The whole process resembles the Europeans explorations since 14th century onwards to new lands via sea-routes with *"we know all attitudes"* and now the people of explored world will learn and adopt from explorers. It is more attuned to looking down on people who do not understand "human rights" as drafted by UN.

The need was to be humbler in their approach while drafting UNHRD which was not actually the case.

11. *"RIGHTS" As an Ego Bridge*

*H*istorically most matured Eastern Philosophies see individual "I" as a restrictive entity.

The evolved purpose of such a view is to allow humans to attain harmony and peace with this world, nature and earth. The whole attempt of more than half of the world culture is to dissolve that "I" and live as a family, community within a social framework.

As we have seen that the Declaration of Human Rights were drafted by those who were heavily influenced by a few centuries of Western education models of science and philosophy, intemperately loaded with human reasoning in finding answers for outward experimentations compared to the Eastern Philosophy and way of looking at life with an inward spiritual growth and transformation.

This startling difference of understanding existing multi-cultural, multi-traditional and multi-geographical and multi-stage of evolutionary worlds in terms of their philosophies, way of life, culture, tradition, history, economic growth and many more factors **were blindly ignored by those drafting the UNHRD**.

What does the concept of Rights do?

"Rights" concept gives a person, a human being – a sense of individuality, a sense of self, and a sense of identity – something that Eastern philosophies have evolved through thousands of years – resting their realization just on the opposite spectrum – *"towards dissolving the sense of self."*

Current "Rights" concept magnifies the "I" of a human being, whereas all the societal life of human being who live in harmony peace in this world try to live in a commune, mingling with others – be it family, relatives, friends and community.

What happens when the "I" grows bigger and bigger – the importance given to oneself and the awareness one gets of claiming one's rights creates conflict with everything - all and every relationships one encounters or comes in contact with.

The above mentioned aspect was totally ignored by the UNHRD committee.

Any person with little common sense will tell that strong bonds and relationships are built on minor self-conceptions and lower self-realized "I"s.

Where does one stop one's own "I" to grow into becoming an EGO booster?

It all depends on one's own awareness of self and the choices one develops and makes in living in harmony and peace with nature, with other organism and species and with fellow human beings.

What if an individual claims rights over everything one has purchased over a piece of land with a price one pays to a seller of land – be it a private or government?

That individual with the concept of "I" and "my ownerships" over something (because of the right given to the person over that piece of land) may exploit that piece of land to such an extent to lay it barren and useless – basically exploiting nature, environment and ruining ecology.

One need to ask – is this approach of "I, My, Mine" - sustainable?

Is that "I" claiming *rights* over something owned by a price – does one believe it to be rightful – really right, and morally right?

The point the author is trying to make is that the model and concept of *rights* has several deep connotations to self boosting EGO trips in the name of claiming one's or a group's *rights*.

If one is not aware *rights* as a concept – **rights** becomes is a bridge that leads to EGO and power and in the end becomes exploitative and abusive of everything around them.

12. UNHRD as A Yardstick

The UNHRD was voted by 48 countries and 8 countries abstained from voting in favor of it.

Most readers of UNHRD will know that UNHRD in its current form may be easily implemented in Western and developed world, because it is written keeping in the evolving Western paradigm.

Each individual is living and growing up within a family, society develops attributes, cultures, thoughts, and ways of life as per their own historical traditions existing from a millennia or more; thus to force on them a moral bondage of UNHRD is not fair by any standards - especially any intelligent person will understands the fact about varied and multi-cultural world we live in today and we can't look at everything with stroke of set of **standardization clauses** like UNHRD.

Any standardization as a concept is itself an abuser of nature, variety, the creativity that exists in this universe and within each individual.

Many nation states had expressed the protection of individual states and their culture to be seen under their respective economic, cultural, traditional and social rights and not solely by the standards and norms defined under UNHRD.

Thus UNHRD is not a yardstick through which one can measure each and every person in the world and their way of life to defend their human rights.

UNHRD is a half-baked pie, that is forced on the world through decades and no one has questioned its fundamentals.

Today UNHRD has become a draconian document that seriously requires urgent revisions and upgrade of emerging world view and liberal mind-sets.

13. Rights as a Governing Concept

A school of thought believes that rights given to an individual as a member of an organization, entity, state, nation, government and/or organization are granted by affiliating with them. These rights are granted by the governing bodies to those individuals and groups.

This school of thought says that any discussion of *rights* beyond this realm is absurd and vacant words, and utter nonsense.

Take for example:

Who gives rights? Either State or Government…

When Government says that every citizen of the country have right to food, housing, clothing, job – it is a right that is granted by the government to its citizens.

Until and unless the government does not lay down these rights for their citizens, members and affiliates – those rights are not bestowed on them.

Mostly these rights are listed in the constitution of each sovereign state.

Thus a person cannot ask beyond their realm of authority who sustains them – demand their rights.

In a family structure, each family has their dos and don'ts and a person or through generations it is defined by the one in power - mostly the elderly person or economic provider in a family.

Who accepts the one in power?

The children – the one who are subjects – either by default with no choice of theirs or by agreeing to those rights given to them in whatever form since childhood are taken for granted.

Can one imagine a human rights organization without the organization defining the rights of its own employees?

Never!

Even the human rights organizations do not solely rely on the UNHRD, because for running an organization those lofty statements are just guidelines and impractical to run day to day affairs even for a human rights organization.

In that sense UNHRD are useless at micro level on daily basis.

Similarly for running a family, a community, a state or a country the UNHRD are useless. One has to develop their own limits of granting human rights privileges to their own subjects for each regional setting culture and tradition.

Thus within the civilized society we live in – "Rights" do not fall over individuals naturally – but have to be decided by a power structure and immediate governing authority be it family, organization or a country state.

Here the author wants to remind the readers again — *remember that any power structure defining rights for their members is a structure that has all the ingredients of being abusive and exploitative of its members.*

A dichotomy in itself…!

14. Human Rights: The Reality Check

Let us understand the UNHRD in the real world we live in today's new millennia.

There is no place in the world where rights are given equally to people except on papers written as UNHRD.

We have failed miserably because each human rights violation and abuse has to be fought for by the victim.

Where on earth the Human Rights as laid down under UNHRD granted?

No Where!

Instead every governing structure has built a mechanistic power system that in itself is abusive; unlike a family power structure that has possibilities of emotions, sensitivities – which are missing in state / nation led protecting structures.

15. Where Have We Failed?

Human Rights – is it an engine of Work in Progress?

This is the argument most Human Rights advocates use to defend what is going on all around the world. Human Rights mandate is a "work in progress".

It is a lame argument.

We ask - for how long?

There are many positive impacts and results because of the push of UNHRD principles – there are thousands of individual cases that have been rescued and saved from torture, detention, imprisonment, execution, persecution, discrimination and there are many laws enacted within a region, a state and a country to protect rights of many vulnerable groups.

Still Human Rights violations do exists and take place. The more awareness about individual rights has resulted in increases in more human rights cases that are reported.

Though the existing system protects the victims, the system itself is burdened by delays, red tape and nepotism, corruption, and impunity.

There are more than ninety per cent of victims who do not even complete the whole process of justice delivery in their life time for a human rights victim.

Yes Human Right may be an engine of *Work in Progress* only under a different impetus than just adapting UNHRD in a state or government in a top-down fashion.

We need to see the whole gamut of socio-cultural-economic factors that have historically influenced the delay and non-delivery of justice to victims of human rights abuses.

One can talk of International Human Rights Legal System that is built to defend and protect individual rights.

To our understanding, a single individual does not have a voice, resources and contacts to reach out to knock the door of that International Legal System.

In that way UNHRD is just a joke for a common person except when educated and made aware – one can quote a clause from UNHRD. That's it!

The biggest problem is that the UNHRD are not legally binding on any sovereign state in the world to hold them accountable. It was just a liberal democratic value obligation for nation states to be part of UNHRD.

Horizontal acceptance across many countries of this declaration has happened, but the vertical implementation within nations is completely lacking in system, values and transparency.

Human Rights are fulfilling an agenda as a show-piece within a country as an obligation to show the international audience of their UNHRD adherence. **This is the biggest failure of UNHRD.**

The local level and grass-root level awareness of international human rights codes and the follow up within the existing local system is what is totally lacking.

Though a so called *idealistic code* is put forward by UNHRD - there is no strong legitimacy within any national legal system without a fight. (In fact the UNHRD clauses are not even idealistic in nature.)

It requires anyone to first educate someone about human rights and the human rights abuses and violations and then the time and resources to fight out the system that is already corrupt. (Remember the tangent case of poor and poverty we read in the second chapter)

The fight of human rights within a country is an uphill task, a large cloud of failure already looming with its over burdened processes.

There are so many short-comings in implementation of an effective system of human rights that it will take another century to enforce them globally.

Till then will UNHRD remain "work in progress"?

16. Freedom, Equality, Dignity

*T*his is what UNHRD plan to ensure for all – Freedom, Equality and Dignity.

How can it be done with a piece of paper that is not a legislative tool of any kind to enforce within a national / country laws and justice, cultural, social, political and economic system?

The task outlined to do that is shown by UN – *"to empower people to demand what should be guaranteed – their human rights."*

How does one empower the whole world to demand human rights for them?

First, they need to be aware that they have rights – some basic rights.

What basic rights?

Once one understands and lists their *rights* down, one knows to compare whether what one is getting is right or wrong in Human Right's context, and also in their culture and tradition context.

If the *rights* is not matching one's understanding of what is rightful; one needs to demands it from some authority who we thinks is there (because the one governing them are authority – selected or elected or by default).

Who is that authority?

One who is more powerful, has more governance, has more resources, money, wealth, influence over others; the one who is as powerful to curtail another person's freedom, equality and dignity.

But we also know that all human structures within any society – family, community, organization, governance are hierarchical structures with people in power governing people with less power.

Until power structures exist – human rights abuse, exploitation will continue.

17. Freedom

*H*uman Rights continuously talks of FREEDOM.

What is Freedom?

We understand when UNHRD talks of *freedom* we know it talks from a western perspective looking outside the human mind and being – less of self-introspection and more of world-criticism.

FREEDOM in UNHRD means '*freedom*' from everything around us existing in this world – so that we can live freely; make our choices freely, to do what we would love to do freely?

We have also seen that human beings under the influence of environment, from birth to the stage where one starts thinking that one is sane enough to make one's own choices – are often dubiously illumined to believe to imitate something they have read, seen, felt and under that influence they are directed with their desires.

Those things around human beings do not let humans to be free from choices of understanding what they want. Some do, but most don't.

Most humans choose their freedom – and immediately get entangled in a cage of their choices – that is self-defeating to their own growth.

Many a times we have seen that one makes many dubious choices in life and feel great about them, without being aware of what they are doing and without realizing the destructive path they have taken – may be for themselves or may be for the world, because they are seen and rewarded by the society and others around them with a price – either monetary or respect or power. Now with this - they are caught into the web of those things and are not free at all.

Such notions of freedom are not what human beings are hoping for. It is like jumping from the hot oil directly into the fire without realizing that the only thing it does is binds you within the realm of your own enhanced self and EGO.

Often humans in realization of freedom get caught within their own self of BIG BIG "I".

Then where is the real FREEDOM?

This non-achieved freedom of "I" is the one that exploits the nature and natural resources and results in human rights abuses.

The Human Rights model under UNHRD enhances the notion of self and cages a personality within the limits of "I" and "Mine".

The purpose of every human being should be how one gains freedom from oneself – from one's "I".

Until one is able to kill one's "I" and free oneself from it – one cannot gain the real FREEDOM.

But UNHRD falls short in understanding that type of freedom.

UNHRD is stuck in a western philosophical view-point and it imposes that "freedom" on the whole world, even the eastern philosophy – that is diametrically opposite to what is believed and mentioned in the UNHRD.

The definition of freedom within UNHRD is a very shallow definition; very superficial. It just skims on the surface to give a wrong notion and sense of freedom – totally artificial.

Dancing, jumping, prancing, singing, running, being excited over nothing, parading, protesting, roaming naked – are the forms of freedom one sees now-a-days humans are superficially aiming for while pursuing the freedom defined under UNHRD. This is the sad interpretation of the whole definition of *freedom*.

Real freedom is when humans are free from their own value of self – the "I".

18. External Freedom

UNHRD also put lots of importance on *freedom* in the way humans expresses their selves. Take the case – every human being should enjoy freedom of speech, freedom of belief and freedom from fear.

It basically means that every human being should have freedom to speak whatever one wants, freedom to choose whichever beliefs one wants and should not have any type of fear in them from doing anything.

These freedoms are considered as high aspiration of every human being.

But are they real freedom?

The declaration falls short to the fact on defining and mentioning that the same freedom of speech can be misused to spread hate, disregard and show contempt towards others.

The freedom of belief may give rise to looking down on others with beliefs different from one's own.

The freedom from fear may lead to getting away with immunity after causing harm and doing whatever one wants to harm and hurt a fellow human being – mentally, emotionally or physically.

Are these permissible under the act of FREEDOM remains unanswered under UNHRD.

Thus no one would agree to such freedom that directly or indirectly harms and hurts others or leads to a chain of events that may be harmful to some innocent species – humans or others – animals, birds, marine and even environment; ultimately resulting in human right abuses.

We will look into further details later in this narrative each human attribute that are different in each one of us and each attribute has the potential to be used as a tool for violating human rights by showing disregard and contempt towards others.

19. Equality

As we understand Equality as defined by Human Rights is: **All human get equal opportunity, pay, treatment and respect in every spheres of life.**

The definition may go a step further, that woman and man are given the same equal status and so with girls and boys. There is no discrimination of any type within and beyond these gender roles – the case here is of the third gender and other genders – coined under various categories of queers is missing.

One needs to see that there is no discrimination because of a person's disability or age or sexual orientation or class, caste, creed, race, color, geographical region and so on...

But in our daily lives we observe discrimination and unequal treatment plated out to various individuals, sections and groups of people. We only need to be sensitive to others around us to watch, realize and feel the insults and humiliation a person goes through because a person in someone's perception and prejudice is considered unequal.

To outline these statements on Equality is fine, but who are the people who discriminate others? Are they you and me? We would not like to believe that. How can we as sensitive being discriminate?

Yet, *inequality* exists within society.

Why?

Because we live in a power oriented hierarchical structures!

Earlier inequality was defined by caste, creed, race, religion, color and now it is directly associated with class; and now class is defined by the wealth one has, how much a person is rich and position one holds and power one has over others.

This is a new form of societal structures modern globalization has presented to us and we fool ourselves and everyone else that within such structures inequality does not exists.

Understand this properly and you will notice that this whole concept of equality is a myth in the current world we live in.

To understand what the author is trying to say — we need to understand the universal nature of things, the world we live in and observe things around us with open eyes sensitively.

Show us any two things that are equal in this world. It is impossible. Even two leaves on the same branch are unequal.

You may say we are talking of equal treatment and not about what is in looks alike. The author understands that.

If we were blind and could not see anything and do not have intellect to realize that this person is getting paid more than me, and that person is holding more power than me or less power than me – than we will understand beyond the looks part of physical appearance.

But the recognition beyond physical attributes – the way a human being is and comes from, belongs to is never ignored by intellect that internally decides one's terms and conditions of equality.

What has happened with time is that we have forgotten to see human beings as unique and this is where the concept of equality under UNHRD fails.

20. Dignity

Dignity is the basic human state of every human being considered worthy to be alive and living, just because they are human beings.

This is how dignity is also seen in the human rights context.

Holding on to the worthiness of understanding dignity and recognizing it – **this whole process of worthiness is in itself a process of valuation, of differentiation, of awareness and of knowing worthiness or unworthiness.**

The question is: Can we remove the tag of dignity and see a human being?

The moment we give recognition of dignity, human mind recognizes everything else that is considered that makes a human being shameful.

Take the case of LOVE. A girl loving a boy and the girl is humiliated for loving the boy, may be by the boy himself or by the society at large.

Now how does dignity fit in this type of case?

How does human right protect the rights of a girl whose basic human dignity is snatched away by this awareness of good and bad associated with an act of love and loving?

Till this association of right and wrong is there in human mind, till the notion of good and bad prevails on judging human beings – **the question and understanding of human dignity is just a "fake" concept.**

The author would go one step further and take forward the example of the girl loving boy.

The author would say that the girl loves the boy so much, that when she finds that her human dignity is crushed and she feels helpless and insulted and rejected by the boy and/or the society is not allowing her to LOVE the boy then either she thinks of ending her life or thinking that she is worthless or would start believing that **she does not care for human dignity if she is allowed to LOVE the boy.**

In the last scenario for this girl, hanging on to the concept and definition of Dignity does not matter a bit.

The girl will say *"I do not want Dignity – I want to LOVE the boy"*

The whole concept of dignity is useless for her as a human being.

She is ready to remove the attire of dignity and the concepts of dignity from anywhere around her – because she sees that dignity is what is coming in her way to be *"FREE to LOVE"*.

The girl surrenders her personal DIGNITY for the sake of LOVE.

The whole aspects of recognizing human dignity by mind is in itself a controlling factor of human beings.

Till that controlling attitude and behavior is prevailing – human dignity will be trampled upon because it is recognized by mind and the society.

The question to ask here is: *Is there any way one cannot recognize the good and bad, the right and wrong?*

That awareness, realization, talent and aptitude are very difficult to achieve for nearly most of human population.

Thus dignity and its definition is good on paper and philosophical discussion, but in bare act of human LOVE and human rights, even the well understood concepts of dignity fails miserably.

21. Peace

Peace is a quiet and calm state of mind. A society that is free from public disturbances and war.

We live in a paradoxical world. Talking of peace looks like a joke, when we see that everywhere around us is in stress, un-calm, disturbed and at war. Any place we go, we see people are worried. Everyone looks stressed out by something from small to big issue of life.

What world we are living in? What world we are making for our future generations?

The news papers are full of crimes and sexual abuse reporting. The news channels survive on scandals, conflict, violence, fake sensational news and in-fights among various people, personalities, nations, sections of societies and nations, across religion, across political parties, across ideologies.

This is what sells, and serves some inner debase need of human consumption – that thrives and is sadistically relishes violence in the society we live in.

Or is it that we are so much fed - day after day for so many years, that we have started enjoying such media sensationalizing everything around us, it has become normal to us to be amidst this state.

A stage is reached that if such state is not around us – we may get un-calmed and stressed.

Where is peace?

The notion of PEACE in UNHRD does not even touch the physically seen peace in the world – let alone it can touch on the inner peace of the mind, body, heart and soul.

After seventy years since UNHRD was drafted in 1947 this concept of peace seems good on paper and has not made a dent in real world that suffers from poverty, and crime and wars, and society is driving human beings to isolations rather than in harmonious, calm peaceful and unifying societies living together.

Today the peace marches are more of protests marches than anything peaceful.

Any march may turn ugly, aggressive and violent at any time – no one knows. It seems to be an accepted way of life around any peaceful gathering.

People have got used to understanding that peace is noise, protest and group activities that are chaotic and noisy and disturbs the normal life.

Sensitive people are amazed – how far human beings have really moved away from the concept of PEACE.

When the experts – learned and educated - coming from developed countries (world powers) talk about PEACE, we can only give them sarcastic smile and turn our head away.

That is the stage of peace we have achieved today – sarcastic look at peace in times of war!

We talk of sustainable development by allowing Corporations, Industries and Factories to encroach forests. Similarly, we seek peace in places where we go there and create nuisance with the natural habitat and environment. Wealthy and Rich enter those peaceful natural spaces with all our technology and gadgets, and roadways, and constructing great lodges and getaways.

Where is sustainability?

Let us evaluate the 60 years of history of UN and what it has done till date to achieve real PEACE except superficial cosmetic touches for meager food and medical supply and care provision for a short while in disturbed and war torn regions?

Not to say that the work of supplying food and medicine need not be done, but UN has just become a post-office and logistical supply chain - rather than permanently policy influential war-curbing situations that give rise to man-made-calamities especially in poor countries because rich countries are eyeing natural resources present in poor countries.

Just a side comment:

Here the author specifically points out on **man-made** *rather than human-made, because the author consciously believes it is the "**Man's**" mind that does everything wrong in this world, and sadly girls and women – in the name of empowerment are imitating everything wrong and bad things that* **men** *have done till now.*

22. Justice

As we understand, **Justice provides equal treatment and rights to all its citizens to access of judicial system so that social and economic benefits reaches the maximum number of people.**

We see today's world, the objective that is to be achieved through UNHRD on justice, remains unfulfilled like many other jargons – that look good to read on paper, and mean well. But the journey of its clauses starts and ends at that.

The world system that is market oriented and globalized, has increased disparities among rich and poor; and gaps of delivering social and economic, political and public benefits to the most needy.

The rich are getting richer and poor poorer. The rich are evading justice and poor are rotting in the system with no means to pull themselves out – mostly as under-trails for decades, many dying in prisons.

The means we are hinting here that further deteriorates justice delivery is wealth, money, bribe, corruption, red-tape, and nepotism – all that work to deliver injustice to most needy and poor sections of the society in poor and developing world.

The government, corporations, industries, crime and banking institutions have formed an uncanny nexus to safe-guard white-collar crimes and grant impunity to the rich under the umbrella of legal framework extended to protect the rich and wealthy with corrupt monetary, financial and banking policies.

Corruption is legalized to such an extent that an individual is arrested for defaulting a minor loan, and industries defaulting millions or billions are written-off and in cases even helped to rehabilitate under sick-unit act in a legal way with disbursement of new loans. One only needs right connection to the people in power in government, banks and decision making bodies.

With time, what we have seen is that theorist and experts have given nuances to the word **"justice"** with adverbs and adjectives and defined, re-defined the notion of justice with several concepts making it a maze of muck that goes deeper and deeper.

No wonder people run away from lawyers, advocate and justice mechanism – that in itself has become a most corrupt system existing in today's modern world.

In coming years, instead of delivering actual real justice the effort is seen to complicate the text around justice for any poor uneducated to understand.

All these looks like intellectual stimulation – but where is actual justice delivered except a few cases here and there?

What is on the rise - Justice or injustice?

See for yourself: existence of unfairness, corruption, dishonesty, falsehood, illegality, injustice, lawlessness, partiality and unethical processes.

The time it takes in years for a poor common person to seek justice is worse than undergoing crucifixion.

The latest trend is that the hiring of Chief Justices in the system is selectively biased towards the ruling party – as per political power and their interest.

Of course there are few cases of justice – but where is justice present in today's world?

23. Born Free

*E*xcept the biological process of man-woman copulating and producing off-springs for the survival of human species on this planet; this process resulting in babies coming out of mother's womb in a form where every baby looks almost same in mind-set at "birth" – naked, crying, vulnerable and helpless.

The freedom of this baby that will grow up as human beings - starts and ends at this point of time, this moment of birth.

The author would even go a step further to say that inside the womb too, the fetus is not FREE. In a sense the fetus is subjected to onslaught of things and thoughts, genes, external environment and food proteins that it is not free to choose.

After birth more so... *is a baby really BORN FREE?*

NO... At every moment the baby is fed with notions of right or wrong – of a life that can be termed as cultural and/ or as per tradition. By the limited exposure a child gets, where is Freedom?

No one is born free or grows up free.

Are human beings who produce off-spring living a life in equality and dignity?

Nor is this case true that as soon as a baby is born – the parents and family attain the status in the world of *equal in dignity and rights?*

Human beings are "Born Free" and "Equal in Dignity and Rights" - both concepts are lofty ideas that hold no grounds in any part of the world that is deeply divided in power, class, caste structures existing through centuries.

A romanticized idea of movie noir and literature!

24. Disregard and Contempt

The two phrases *disregard and contempt* of human beings - resonates the foundation commitment of UNHRD

How does disregard and contempt really happen? What are its root causes?

When does a human being start disregarding another human being?

When and how does a human being see with contempt towards other human beings?

As one understands, for one to disregard another human being – one has to have a notion of "I am better" than them.

How does one get such a notion?

It happens when one perceives that they have something more in them. In real sense, may be or may be not...!

It mostly could be own perception – right or wrong. But they believe that they have something better than others to see towards them with contempt.

What could be that *something better?*

Let us try to list down a few:

Knowledge, education, information, money, wealth, money, bank balance, the property one own, the place (region) they are born, the religion they are born in, the caste, class, community they are born in, the people and friends they have, the people with whom they enjoy company, looks - the perceived beauty of oneself, the attribute within them which is praised by others and they see not present in others and the notion of superior choices they make and the list may go on and on.

The list is unending...

Every one of us is different in the above criteria; and **from where that notion comes that**:

My knowledge is better than someone else's knowledge? My education is better than their education? My religion is better than others, so on and so forth...

Each or any of the above criteria can be used as looking down on others with disregard and contempt.

The basic and most subtle attribute amongst all these that makes a person dislike something in others is – **being indifferent to someone's interest in you or hating someone – just like that!**

Most people do not go deep or self-introspect into knowing their likes or dislikes, their indifference or their hate.

In the garb of freedom, people are safe to do what they prefer and walk away with disregard and contempt, make fun and laugh off others without knowing the type of human right violation they are indulging in.

All this behavior emerges from the notion of *"I have something better".*

The author is also aware that not all people with a notion of "I" are bad people, but the intrinsic value of "I" carries with it much baggage and that is one humans need to aware of.

The key to understand disregard and contempt is the concept of "I"

How to stop such behavior?

The world cannot provide each and every individual with similar or same type of factors mentioned above NOR world can make a person with awareness of *"No I"*

Till "I" is there within individuals – how much one tries – the human rights violation will happen starting with disregard and contempt towards other human beings based on what the "I" has and what one sees the other person does not have.

The "I" is the limiting factor within all human beings that disallows them to see the cosmic universality of the world we live in.

25. Reason

UNHRD claims that *all human beings are given reason and we all should act with one another in a spirit of brotherhood* [sic]. Sorry, they should have used a better word - kinship is more suitable – as a gender neutral language.

The very base of Article 1 of UNHRD fails to recognize the fact that the moral of right and wrong and the reason to justify individual acts based on that conscience is the one thing that is causing most of the human rights and injustice problems in the world.

UNHRD assumes people will have *good conscience* – meaning people will live in harmony with everything around them as a value of life.

Bad conscience may mean a person creating disharmony with fellow human beings and natural environment. Bad conscience also carries living a futile and useless existence without any human values associated with it of "what one is doing is right or wrong?"

From where does values of right and wrong come?

It is through one's upbringing, the environment humans live in and the environment – family, friends, culture and tradition one follows and grows up in.

Each value learned has a logical, rational and scientific reasoning behind it – why one does what one does – especially when it is learned as being part of the bigger society that accepts whatever a child is taught.

This is how the conscience of human beings takes birth – within reason of right and wrong one has learned through growing up.

If one goes deep down the essence of evolution of society – one will find that the basic foundation of all human teachings always **LOVE is at the core of the building of values around right and wrong and it will remain so forever.**

But this fact is mostly forgotten by layers of ritual and traditions, and practices, desires of success and wealth - that smudge the reality of life and living.

There is the rise of reason that many a times clouds the senses on this basic essence of nature and reality called *"LOVE"*.

With reason over-powering a person and many a times mind confronting LOVE - the basis of human existence gives rise to EGO and later, if it remains unchecked – it gives rise to super EGO, ultimately leading to violation of rights of many kinds.

EGO builds up the "I" and super EGO builds up the "Power structures" around that "I"

Every human has a germ of that "I" and EGO within them to a certain extent, that is vehemently protected by reason and mind.

EGO and super EGO cannot exist within itself without causing human rights violation.

The reason that creates havoc is a reason that is exactly, dramatically opposite that opposes LOVE.

The human with Ego and Super EGO wants and expects to be paid attention to; rather than a human who wants to have conscience with reason of the basic premises of existence and wants to LOVE others.

Being LOVED by others and LOVING others is the key difference between bad and good conscience respectively.

Let us remember that both are backed by reasons of different and opposite kind.

We will again talk of conscience later in the book. Wait a while!

26. *Inner Voice*

*T*his is a concept that is not mentioned in the UNHRD. But it is important to understand this concept to understand fully the concept of conscience.

'Inner voice' is much different from reason and conscience.

A lot of times, in the time of doing and making choice of an action – people use reason and conscience, that are developed and gained through living and growing up, **whereas "inner voice" is something that is inert within human beings – that makes us feel uneasy when we harm someone or someone is hurt, when someone cries because of one's act, when someone suffers because of what one has done something.**

How to differentiate between inner voice and conscience?

It is difficult.

Conscience is always related to an incident in one's life that makes us feel a similar emotion like understanding right/ wrong and justice/ injustice – but it is always strongly backed by a past incident and a reason of right and wrong associated with one's memory.

Whereas *inner voice* is not backed by any incident of neither one's times nor it has any reason to fall back to; but being aware of that inner voice – makes a person alert of right and wrong without any due reason to it or memory associated with any past incident.

A controlling action of family, friend, teacher, society that curb any type of freedom gives rise to non-conceptual level of consciousness backed by incident and reason in terms of panic, fear and guilt associated with doing some acts.

For example, many people grow up with the fear to *LOVE* someone; or fear of *being LOVED* by someone – because something had happened in their childhood – an incident which they remember that restricts them – stops them from a beautiful natural human emotion like LOVE.

Finally when a person grows up with such baggage of being stopped to do something – the person grows up with feeling of isolation and rebellion within oneself. Either a person becomes a strong critic or uses sarcasm to cover up one's own short-coming with humor and cynicism.

Associating one's act with punishment given to them and scolding received and labeled as misdeeds - **builds up the conscience and reason of a person** but it is quite different from the concept of inner voice.

Many acts of such moral conscience are seen while growing up under religious teachings of rights and wrongs that are backed by a strong reason – why one should do something or why we should not do something.

Maturing of conscience is a process and from *conscience backed by reason* to *conscience backed by inner voice* **takes a life-time.**

Conscience in different people may lead to different valuation or right and wrong and / or feelings of guilt even when faced with the same type of event and situation.

Whereas inner voice – if one is able to listen to it – remains the same across human beings.

But the concept and understanding of inner voice is more meta-physical in nature and thus conscience is used in UNHRD that can be backed by reason.

Not to say that conscience is always right – it can be learned to be different from inner voice and **conscience can be utterly wrong and damaging at many times.**

27. *Universal Respect*

Promotion of universal respect for one another is the foundation of UNHRD.

Universal respect for everything around us comes from the fact that a person understands that one lives in harmony and peace with one another and not with disregard and contempt.

Respect of a human being is in whatever and however state - of physical, mental, emotional, psychological being – the person is respected for what one is.

The above mentioned statement defines **universal respect**.

As a principle everyone should follow it. Those who wander away from this principle are mainly due to the fact of their childhood problems.

One cannot laugh at, look down upon, make fun of and disrespect a person for anything they do, speak and think – whatever values and conscience, reasons and logic they hold that are different from yours.

With perceived differences a person should not be prosecuted for what one believes is, nor the person should be insulted, isolated, humiliated for being exactly as a person is and feels.

If a person loves you – you need not punish the person because that person LOVES you.

That is the type of universal respect one talks about while talking of human rights.

But how many people we see practice such basic courtesy of respect for fellow beings?

28. Common Understanding

United Nations expects a certain level of common understanding of universal human rights.

As we have seen the differences – though not so closely or deeply as it needs to be seen – it is impossible to expect that at any level with the diversity – geographical, cultural, religious, traditional, economic, social, and environmental and many more – there is chance or possibility of attaining any common understanding of the intricate meaning and understanding of human rights.

The author assumes that at a superficial level one can understand what HUMAN RIGHTS means. But if one accepts that and goes ahead leading a normal with the sense that everything is all right – it will lead to tremendous amount of distortion in complicating the existing human rights narrative.

In UNHRD there are so many idealistic assumptions and presumptions of a simple and linear world we live in – which is not the case in real world we live in.

To attain common understanding of human rights at deeper level – that covers all the concepts and its understanding is difficult and impossible.

Whereas, going ahead with superficial understanding of human rights is disastrous trap-hole that would keep human beings busy for no reason. Also it has a potential to further distort and complicate the individuals and families and societies.

29. *Entitlement – I*

Can a global body like UN entitle the whole of humanity with all the rights mentioned on a piece of paper?

Especially when that body (United Nations) does not have any influence or legal, traditional, religious standing to touch on lives of individuals in different remote geographical regions and cultures where entitlements vary every hundred kilometers?

Unlike western societies that are built with no cultural and evolutionary history of thousands and millennium years – and just has about 500-700 years of history to fall back on; they fail to understand this very fact by **giving entitlement to the whole world under one umbrella in a top down manner** is not the solution – even though it implies taking signatures of every nations to comply by UNHRD clauses.

At times, one feels what a group of stupid persons could agree on such a thing and do not people give a little bit of serious thought to what they are doing – (even with their noble intentions?) in forcing the whole of human society with such commandments of sorts that are impossible to implement or monitor anyways.

UNHRD also states that there should be no distinction being made based on political, jurisdiction, and international status of country or territory to which a person belongs – either independent, trust, non-self-governing, or limiting sovereignty.

The things they have surely missed in UNHRD narrative are evolved religion, culture and traditions.

May be while drafting UNHRD, the drafting committee was in too much hurry or so much into different political philosophical governing structures that they totally forgot that there exists thousands other more localized driving forces beyond political philosophy that influence and guide human mind, their cultures and traditions.

This is a big missed gap in drafting the UNHRD.

We will look at ENTITLEMENT again in part 2, after looking into some other concepts of Human Rights

30. Right to Life

*I*t is a grand thought and noble intention to lay down a declaration stating that everyone has a right to life, but without building the system and process for such implementation – it is totally futile.

In today's times, when human and animal lives are taken (killed) by frenzy for no rhyme or reason by any sorts of forces that are unrelated to the victim whose life is lost is so disturbing to digest. The case in point is drone attacks and bombardments on areas by powerful nations in the name of PEACE.

The victims dying are unknown entities in far off geography that may not be ever related or accused of crimes for which they are killed by drones attacks and bombardments.

Crimes, accidents and failure in providing help of any kind by the government in times of natural calamity, wars, daily human to human conflict and confrontation that takes innocent lives of millions every day – who is responsible for all these?

Our modern times - the times we live in!

There are factors like economic, social, political and regional that takes away the right to life of thousands of people every day. Who is responsible for that?

By just writing **Right to Life** – is it going to change anything?

What we have seen is that things are going from bad to worse daily – every day with growing modern times.

31. Liberty to a Person

*L*iberate means setting someone free from imprisonment, slavery and oppression.

Is a person liberated to do what one wants to do? Live where one wants to live in this world? Travel and stay where on wishes? Is a person liberated to live peacefully without fear?

In today's times, humans are guarded and monitored by surveillance and vigilance of all types, mostly by the government.

Living (even with a free will) under such a dreadful environment of policing is not liberty.

There is no individual privacy existing in today's time - especially when technology has over-powered even our day to day transactions that are stored and when needed accessed and monitored by the government; where every key-stroke of yours is monitored somewhere in building your online identity with internet providers and in many cases – your life-history by government. Every individual is given a number and monitored from birth to death. **This is no liberty!**

People may have been brain-washed to believe that living under the vigil of web-cameras at every street corners of the cities is a way of life in liberty but it is not living with liberty but living under stress and fear of being hawked by crime.

When a person's private life and online transactions are dubiously monitored by cookies and cache; with vigor to know our bank balance and income tax and purchasing habits – that is not a life of a liberated person.

A tracking system of human beings from birth to death – from passport to human ID number to multiple identity proofs to finger prints – is not a life of a liberated human being. It is a life of an imprisoned person always carrying an identification number who is made to believe that the person is liberated.

Any reasonable thinking person will challenge this whole notion of false security and vigilance as a dubious claim of liberation to a person.

The UNHRD does nothing to address these emerging issues as protecting the privacy of an individual and providing justice under human rights violations.

32. Security of Person

Security means being free from danger and / or any threat.

Where is security of a person, especially for those who are affected by crimes, economic, social, cultural vacuums, famine, droughts, ecological natural environment exploitation leading to climate change endangering security of lives – animal and human throughout the planet?

In such a scenario how can one provide security to a person, a group, a community except superficial cosmetics things?

When the world is surrounded by various kinds of insecurities hence there is a natural desire to create a sense of security.

That is why the need for security.

Safe and security against crime, robbery, molestation, rape, kidnapping on a personal level and internal riots, disturbances, economic and social in-securities on other side at national level; whereas on international borders there are in-securities on defending the national borders.

Everyone tries to create security of some kind around them. **People have only known to live with a sense of insecurity around them. People are always on an alert.**

The Government of a region, state and country are given this UNHRD human right mandate to provide security.

Whatever governments have done till now, they have not been successful to give security to most people. Everyone is living under a sense of threat at public places.

Philosophically one needs to understand that a person is only completely secured when one is dead in a grave.

Only in grave nobody can harm anyone, on alight note - people are already dead there!

That is why people are trying to create the same security of a graveyard in real life – feeling secured by money, by power, by prestige, by social conformity, by belonging to a herd, by being part of the family, a nation and so on.

How much ever government provides a sense of security - people are creating as many barriers between one another in the fear of unknown.

Everyone is forgetting that the more one gets involved in creating security around a person, a community, a society, a religious identity and a nation – the more insecure, imprisoned and dead that society will become.

UNHRD works on that logic of pushing cordons of security around every one – thinking that is going to create freedom, but in actuality it is just creating prisons and false sense of comfort.

It is a dichotomy that **one needs to create freedom by providing security – that is impossible**.

Either you have freedom or you have security. If you have security – there is no real freedom. If there is freedom, there has to be a life with no security.

Security is an illusion in today's world.

The world has moved so far away from the real sense of freedom (the one that gives inborn security like a bird flying – *wings in flights*) that type of security is now impossible to have among people in the world who are free from danger and threat.

We have reached a world of no returns. With time, the layers of security, scrutiny, walls are going to increase and suffocate all of us; not only at national, societal but at personal level too – there is enormous distrust due to this fear of insecurity between two individuals too.

UNHRD aiming for such a society has only understood life, freedom and security as superficial as a shallowest pond compared to the deep ocean.

33. *Slavery & Servitude, Slave Trade*

UNHRD clearly states *"No one shall be held in slavery or servitude and slave trade shall be prohibited in all forms"*

Slave means a person who is considered an owned property of someone else.

Slavery means the state of being a slave accepted as a social practice and norm

Servitude means the state of being a slave under a person, an institution and may also be for a particular time period

Slave Trade means procuring, detaining, transporting, and selling of humans

With these definitions let us understand the efficacy of human rights law against slavery under UNHRD.

The type of slavery that existed in past centuries where slaves could be owned and killed by owners at will – **of course such type of mass-slave trade does not exists today.**

But in today times illegal human trafficking mainly associated with commercial sex trade where children, girls and women are trafficked and there are severe inhuman abuses that may lead to the victims of such trafficking / slavery being killed or dying during the process of transit.

In today's world, in most nations under current legislation it is very difficult, almost impossible to legally keep slaves, slavery or servitude or slave trade.

Yet modern slavery is defined and exists in various other forms illegally:

- **Bonded labor** including child labor
- **Domestic service** – overtime, under-pay, poor working conditions
- **Forced begging** – an urban phenomenon run by mafia
- **Commercial sexual exploitation** – trafficking of boys, girls, man and woman

Some other forms that are hidden and do not fall under illegal slavery but still do exist are:

- **Forced marriage** – mainly marriage of people under legally permissible age due to existing historically accepted social traditions
- **Psychological slavery** – obligatory behavior that restricts freedom of individuals to do what they want to do - due to their obligation towards some power authority
- **Liberal slavery** – is a more complex form where future benefits (that may never happens or materialize) – as better pay, promotion, better job, better working environment, holidays and vacation benefits, or threats of loss of current job, or terrified by line-manager's anger, demands and

demeanor, or working in a place that is shown to mentally coerce an individual to work or working at a place that resembles a cult organization or working as a volunteer or an intern with no payments.

- **Undefined Slaves to wealth** and money makes human beings do things below basic human rights standards without realizing it and many a time humans intentionally subject themselves and others to short-medium-term of de-humanizing work environment.

We will not discuss this in detail here, but would like to make a point that UNHRD does not consider the new emerging slavery routes, ways and methods where humans are slaves to wealth, money and power that ultimately drive human right violations and much of it remains un-noticed under the current definition of slavery in UNHRD.

34. Torture Cruelty Punishment

*U*NHRD's **main focus is to highlight the physical torture inflicted on victims by those in power.** A lot of international human rights activities focus on this **grave type** of human abuse.

There are other tortures that are also covered under the broad definition of torture, like - **mental, psychological and emotional** that many people undergo in their daily life, but the gravity of them are not as serious to life and as threatening as **physical torture** that may even kill a human being if not rescued and saved.

The more developed the economy and the higher the intelligence of human mind and thus the type of tortures covered under this UNHRD clause will differ.

Developed and rich economies are more inclined to mental, psychological and emotional torture cases rather than physical torture (surely there are exception like Abu Ghraib prison) - that would come as inhuman treatment meted by individuals in power.

Remember again, the fulcrum of all inhuman and human rights violation is POWER – a position of power.

We find those fulcrums of power all around us – implemented through instruments like- salary, position one holds, caste, class, wealth, property and you may define it in as many ways you think like.

Till power equation exists in human society – human rights violation will exists.

Only way to abolish human rights violation is to remove power structures.

Even in a human rights organization too, power structures are given emphasis and we need to start there to show change by removing power structures - **especially in human rights organizations, just to lead by example.**

35. Right to Recognition

*E*veryone – living or dead – has a right to be recognized under law locally, nationally and internationally; even in the case if they are missing or disappeared from the society.

This is one interpretation of the right to recognition. If anyone feels that they or someone they have known – living or dead is/was subjected to inhuman treatment one can seek justice for their human rights abuse under the law irrespective of the person is physically present or not.

No law in the world can deny this fact of right to recognition of a human being seeking justice for their rights.

Here, the curious case would be of those who do not fall under the legal bracket of recognition.

The case here could be for those who are denied certain rights or privileges under a government just because the history has not treatment them as likely beneficiaries of such privileges.

As an example we will refer here to the thousands pension cases that appear of Nazi volunteers under World War II Hitler regime - who are denied pension in their old age.

Even if these Nazi volunteers were not directly involved in any inhuman act of World War- II – that too which happened more than five decades ago, should they be denied of a basic human rights as any old person of the society?

Those who feel left out of the system due to any historical, geographical, cultural reasons and feel vindicated by local, national, regional or international law can seek refuge under the declaration of *"right to recognize"* to build up a case.

Having said this – let us also be aware that there are millions of people who are un-recognized because of their historical baggage, the place they belong, their caste, creed, race, religion and various other factors that deny them basic rights to entry to a place, to basic necessities of life – food, clothing and shelter.

With the focus on high-profile society of today, many individuals are left out or even not recognized as part of the society.

Main-stream media is the best example to mention here – how the apathies of marginalized groups living away from urban conglomerate are hardly or never covered on prime time media.

There is a very high correlation between the more far the place from the head-quarter of urban centers, the less coverage of those human rights violations and abuses presented, shown, covered or discussed by the main-stream media.

The UNHRD's reach in creating awareness is not enough to bring equality and justice in poor person's life in providing legal and needed benefits that are rights based.

Why?

Because they are not recognized by bureaucracy or negligently overlooked by those in powers; thus this **right of recognition is very important – but under-utilized**.

36. *Entitlement – II*

*U*nder any law every human being is entitled to basic necessities of life and nobody can deny those things to be 'given' to them, irrespective of their regional or geographical birth place, caste, creed, class, religion, education qualification, gender, age and so on.

But what happens if entitlement is tied up with capabilities?

If the government or those in power define that this is entitled for only those who fit in a list of certain criteria, many people would not be entitled to even apply or seek privileges or position, rations, jobs etc.

The key case of example is women in some cultures who are denied basic education and social mobility within the culture due to the tradition and their being a woman.

Should entitlement flow to those who are not considered capable because of conservative (restrictive) tradition and culture?

Many human rights advocates would say– "All entitlements should flow to everyone irrespective of any criteria." That is why at places some caste, tribes and in some countries woman are given affirmative quotas to be part of the process that makes the system reflect equality.

Let us take another example here – Job.

What happens when a person who applies for a job is from an institute that does not provide quality education and exposure required for performing a job?

Should that person be given a job?

OR the other way around, what one would say to the company that does not even know the difference between high-rank and low-rank institutes of quality and reputed education while selecting a candidate and looks everyone with the same lens.

When we talk of entitlement this is a Catch-22 situation.

Especially in UN – the one who preaches of entitlements - you will find ghettos of a particular clan, caste, community, nationality, geographical representation and class grouping together and getting prime posts and jobs in UN. The job and recruitment mafia at UN works in the most systematic corrupt way – even after layers of transparency and screening mechanism.

Though UN will deny it, but it is true. Those who have worked in UN know what happens and how a person who is already selected before advertisement gets the job at the end of the whole transparent quality process of external advertisement and recruitment.

UN promotes this crony culture year after year in favoring government servants – one of the most corrupt practices existing in UN. In doing so, UN denies the basic human rights entitlements to many who might fit the bill even with capabilities.

This is a very tricky issue to pin-point and expose because the system is geared to be corrupt, to cover up transparency to non-transparent, legal to un-officially legalize, open yet hidden and kept secretive that – especially in places like UN and World Bank (WB), though they may lay the process and system in place – but be sure that it could be perpetually programmed to deny entitlements to those who do not fit into the mind-set of those in power – game of recruitment.

In many UN posts you will find people who look from Bangladesh, India, Africa, Pakistan or any other developing countries, but they are just clones of the ideology that match western educated minds. Physically they look like they are representing their particular nationalities but their inner core, thinking process and "standards" is just of a western, rich, developed country mind-state. **Sad state of affairs at UN – the one who proclaims to be the guardian of development and human rights!**

"Survival of fittest" though a good theory to explain human growth – it is laid down with every inhuman treatment we can think of. More so is the case when we talk of competitive market economy where the fittest survive.

Kindly remember, that **survival of fittest is the one that has brought the world to where it is right now, where the planet is standing on verge of extinction** – especially millions of flora and fauna and thousands of endangered species, and the poor and indigenous population who do not fit into the "STANDARD" definition of market driven society are either eliminated or killed or brought to the brick of non-existence till they disappear from this earth.

In such scenarios ENTITLEMENT is very useful.

One can see its application in everyday life – either in social or professional dealings or any daily interactions with people.

The author highlights to the reader that if one is aware and leading a working life, meeting people – one may at least notice in their career an entitlement being denied around them to someone whom one thinks fit the bill of entitlement perfectly.

People may justify it as a play of fate and destiny, but do not believe them because it has germinated from the corrupt intentional minds to cheat people and deny people of proper entitlements.

That time one should be aware and one will notice that the organizational system is skewed to defend those denied of entitlement because of profit or performance motives. A reason strongly used against hiring women for many roles and jobs that they are equally capable of.

Like in the developmental sector - in under-developed and developing countries – the work for poor are done by wealthy higher caste individuals, and in countries like India most big Non-Governmental Organizations (NGO) are headed by the elite Brahmin caste –which is shameful because there are many better people who come from poor communities who know the ground realities and are more entitled to perform the same and the chances are that they start the work with better compassion and understanding of real exploitative issues.

Even the work of poverty is not left untouched by the wealthy and higher caste.

The hierarchy, the position one comes from, the power one gathers through their social status and education; the caste and class, wealth and power make some people being perceived to gain better entitlement even though they do not deserve the same.

Here we are not talking of performance, but entitlement irrespective of capabilities.

Give a thought to this very important issue around 'rights' – very useful to see the world around you with totally new perspective.

37. Effective Remedy

*E*very individual should have access to effective remedy.

Effective remedy means that an individual's human rights violation is address by the local government to the some satisfaction of that individual who has suffered human rights abuse.

For effective remedy the local government needs to have proper laws that are equipped to address human rights violations.

For a government to have laws – they should be aware of the need of such laws. If the law is there, the victims should know the process of accessing such laws.

The law in itself should have all the processes and systems clearly outlined that comprehensively cover effective remedies to wide variety of cases on human rights violations.

These remedies may range from punishment to violator, to payment to victim for violation, or any help to relocate, rehabilitation, professional services, training, employment, legal support or any other means possible that will satisfy the victims or the family member of the victim.

Obviously there may be many cases where the victim feels unsatisfied with the justice around the case of human rights violation.

It is important to check here that whether in the name of justice the government is indulging in another human rights violation of some sort or not, because that is what is demanded by the victim. Such situations should be avoided.

But when a victim genuinely feels unsatisfied by the effective remedy under the law of the state – what options does one have to knock the door of higher human rights authorities above the national level highest judicial body – in most cases the Supreme Court?

The Presidential or Premier's intervention to look into the case is one way.

Is there any way a victim can knock the door of International Justice Courts for help?

Under current UNHRD, the answer is "NO" because only nations and states are eligible to appear before the International Court to submit a case.

International laws do not have any jurisdiction to address individual case or case of any other organization.

One way to continue the struggle to seek justice is to create campaigns individually or with the help of non-government or civic society organization or a group or community who think that justice has not been delivered in this case to achieve an effective remedy.

The problem with the justice system in many parts of the world is the time it takes to reach a state of effective remedy. In most cases this may take many years before the victim or family of victims are satisfied with the remedial measure offered by the government.

Though it is impossible to lay down variants of cases that lead to a human rights violation, but an effective and transparent institutional process in addressing the victim's plea in particular time frame that speeds up the whole process is necessary.

38. Government's Role in Violation

$\mathcal{A}$rticle number 9 of UNHRD talks of stopping a person legally by means as broadly described below:

Arbitrary Arrest*:* When no reason is given and a person is arrested, that terms as arbitrary arrest.

Detention*:* When a person is detained for a certain period of time is called detention

Exile: When a person is barred from home country, this constitutes exile.

Normally these three types of scenarios and definitions are observed with respect to the state and/ or government using the legal route to arrest, detain or exile a person.

In such cases the UNHRD defines it as violations of human rights.

In every country to prevent individual and / or group protesting against the state means of '*stopping a person*' are used by governments with an assumption that if the person is not stopped the situation may lead to violence and harm to others and / or damage to public property.

In most cases this is misused by state government when it is implemented; mostly without giving any prior notice or any information or court orders to anyone. Such actions are not right or correct in any human framework.

The cases of human rights violations become dire when the arbitrary arrest, detention and exile extend to periods that are considered alarming by any legal standards.

The author opines that any arrest, detention of exile over and above 24 hours should be viewed as human rights abuse.

The reason given by government is: For safely measure such laws are passed and given sanctions to maintain peace and harmony in the society; especially in this new world order where terrorists are feared by every nation to strike at will.

The role of UN as a moral authority to provide pragmatic, practical and realistic solution is very limited.

Individual rights are curb to a great extend under this type of *'stopping a person'.*

Many people who are detained, arrested and exiled disappear and some are never ever found again. Many times Human rights organization and activists claim that this is an easy way to kill and eliminate a human being without any judicial process.

So any government, nation or state indulging in any of the above – arrest, detention or exile becomes human rights violator.

Thousands of human right cases are documented that show that most government overlooks UNHRD in protecting their nation and UN stands helpless to protect or even influence those governments.

This problem is so deep rooted with national jingoism and diverse radical differences, that to find a solution within current framework of modern society is almost impossible.

39. Fair

The word "**fair**" is used just once in the entire document of UNHRD. But let us understand that - **FAIR is a very important word.**

What does fair mean?

In context of human rights - simple and easy definition to understand is **"to treat people equally without favoritism or discrimination"**

Now who defines the psychology of a person who is listening to another person fairly, and / or does fairness match with the definition of "fair" of the person who is heard?

So when fairness principle is discussed we are looking in one case and two definition of "fair".

"Fair" as defined by the one in power – the violator and "fair" as defined by the victim, the one whose human right is violated.

There are so many aspects of fair and fairness when we discuss it under human rights context.

We will list down the points below that routinely are looked into while reviewing legal cases. It highlights that – especially in human right violations cases, one need to re-looked violations more closely with more details.

o Does everyone really get access to an expert lawyer or a court room or a hearing in front of a judge to seek justice?

o Even if one gets access to justice to some extent, who will give guarantee for the person who is hearing the case of human rights violation – is independent of bias, prejudice etc.

o **It is assumed that the person hearing a case is independent and impartial and one has to just believe it blindly and accept it.** But no human being – leave alone a judge can be given such certification of being independent.

The fact remains that most judges are not independent and impartial. **Whatever said every living individual carries a baggage of past that sub-consciously and unconsciously works while interacting with someone in personal and professional matters.**

This is the fact of the society we live in, the society we grow up in, and the society that nurtures our values, morals and conscience.

Humans are not machines who are programmed. **Expecting an independent and impartial judge is just a myth.**

o Fair is when the hearing of a case is heard within a reasonable time limit.

The number of under-trails in the world is thousands times more than the ones who have access to even one hearing in the court. Of course this may not be true in developed and wealthy nations.

o   Who and how can one set a time limit for hearing a case and at which levels of court's hierarchy – district, state, national, high, supreme or international court.

o   Most poor people spend their entire life time running from pillar to post for their case of seeking justice or to prove their innocence to live a normal life without a stigma.

o   Fair means transparency, access to all the information pertaining to the case without anything under-hand or hidden.

o   It is a hard and difficult thing to achieve with layers of laxities in investigation and its reporting, but that is what is expected from a fair justice in human rights – a thorough investigation and reporting.

o   It is important that enough time should be given to the case for a fair hearing and trial – the person seeking justice should never feel that the case is curtailed due to pressure of other cases and lack of time.

The paradox appearing here is that though we want justice in a particular time frame - time limit is a systemic loop-hole that should not exist while delivering fair justice.

o   Fair is when any questions, doubts, decisions (subjective or objective) are taken in the case only after proper reasoning based on logic and rational and above all with humanity, care and compassion - communicating the same to the victim as and when the case evolves.

o   Fair as in a human rights case should have access to equally qualified and experienced experts of law and justice – that itself is the first fair step to be taken by the law

o   In all fairness – when any point is discussed on the case – the parties, especially the victim should be present to listen and have an opportunity to react to whatever is implied out of the case in terms of what is correctly understood.

o   Fair is only when the case gives open and transparent access to public (except in cases of confidentially for protecting a victim's privacy due to sexual nature of the violation) – immediately or in future through proper documentation records – written, audio or video as systems provide to be fair to all the parties.

So how is being "fair" applicable in human rights context?

It is easy to lay down the above mentioned points. It makes a good reading, but where is the practical ease to fulfilling this clause of UNHRD?

Even though **'fair and fairness'** are very important principles **it is a shame that FAIR word is used just once in the entire UNHRD and the aspects of conceptually underlining the details are kept vague.**

Vagueness is the striking feature with most words and concepts used under UNHRD.

Vagueness brings complexity in the interpretation and becomes a chaotic ball of inextricable tangle of threads of words.

The more one tries to untangle it – the more inextricable it becomes – that is the current position of the human rights laws in today's world.

The list given above is not an exhaustive list of tracking "fair" and "fairness" in human rights context. But any human rights justice process over-looking or missing a single point is a violation in itself of UNHRD's "fairness" clause.

40. Tribunals

*T*ribunal means a body established to settle disputes.

Under UNHRD the application of Tribunals is for cases of dispute around human rights violation between the one who is accused of violation and the victim who has suffered human rights violation.

Like regular criminal cases, what happens is that Human Rights law too is driven by black and white evidences and has taken a shape of mechanical and too much water-tight-case-based evidence approach that has taken away the humanity, humane and compassion aspects from the human rights dialogue, especially when we see the case from the perspective of the victim.

Many may surely argue against a less stringent mechanism to look into human rights cases. But just imagine, when we are talking of human rights cases, we are dealing with human beings and if we are making a tribunal to look into such cases that only comprise of lawyers and experts of law - *what we will end up with?*

But sadly that is exactly what many human rights tribunals have become.

In tribunals there should be lawyers who are experts on laws relating to social issues, employment, economic, migrations and other fields.

Instead there are always a group of judges - retired Chief Justices - who are members or heading such tribunals.

Even when the tribunal invites a human rights person – the person is in most likelihood a lawyer; (because a person needs to know the game of law and its working) which defeats the whole purpose of representing the diverse and pluralistic world we live in.

Though by training a good lawyer with years of experience looks into every aspect, but at the same time after years of process and system driven approach, lawyers due to such training and mechanistic experience tend to bring just one kind of automated outlook into the tribunal, (follow the rules, laws and procedures) and that such behavior and attitude should be avoided, especially in human rights cases.

Establishing a tribunal with a good composition is convenient with respect to local legislation and justice system, but it would be better if people who are experts from different fields and women are also invited apart from judges and lawyers.

This would make the tribunal more humane and would look at cases outside the box of justice system.

Though under UNHRD tribunal is called impartial tribunal; but in most cases with existing hierarchy of powers and positions of Chief Justices and Judges inside the tribunal - the game of power comes into picture where the word of the one who is experienced and senior-most in power is considered important and that leads to the apathy of partiality.

In all cases such tribunals this should be avoided.

The need is to make the composition of tribunal fair and non-hierarchical to grant equality and impartiality.

41. Criminal and Crime

Criminal means a person who has committed a crime.

Crime means an action or omission what is considered an offence by law.

Offence is annoyance, resentment, perceived insult and / or attacking someone.

Once one of the above happens it may result in human rights violation of some kind and needs to be addressed with human rights law.

The one who commits such or any offence that degrades human rights of an individual is termed as a criminal.

Not everyone arrested for an action / offence is a criminal. The person can be wrongly accused. Thus a criminal is not called a criminal until the person is proved of the crime.

If there is out-right recorded evidence available in real time footage of crime that cannot be defended by the accused and the team of lawyers - the case becomes much stronger against the accused 'criminal'

Otherwise the long procedure of evidence building of different types – forensic, eye-witness, physical evidences at crime scene, documents, electronic – audio/visual recorded, real, circumstantial, polygraph, psychological tests, etc. is used to prove a crime and frame the accused under various penal codes of legal laws.

The frequency of same crime recorded earlier for the same person is considered as **habitual offender** and the chances to prove the crime and prove the accused criminal becomes easier.

All these aspects are taken into consideration for bringing criminal charge against a person for a crime otherwise any slackness in building full-proof evidence may lead to punishing a wrong person for a crime one has not committed and that would mean violating human rights of that person.

Poor evidence building at the crime scene also delays the whole process of justice. This should be avoided.

The author takes liberty to stretch the argument to more idealistic and philosophical level to make the educative discourse provocative.

Those who are called criminal are not born criminal and they are made criminal by the circumstances and society. Like blindness some person inherits genes of crime, and as we do not punish a blind person for being blind, how can one punish a criminal for committing crime.

42. Penal

*W*hen under a legal system of any group, society, community, region or a nation, a person is a prescribed punishment it is considered penal or charged with penal offence or an offence that is punishable.

The basic problem with punishment when it is mentioned in UNHRD should not be accepted because punishment to human being in itself is a human rights violation.

Anyone who is learned will know that punishment never cures or repairs a human being. Take the example of a child that is punished, anyone will tell you that punishment leaves scars on the psyche of a child that grows up to be a person - that scar remains throughout the life.

Punishment to a child can be - an oral scolding, a slap, a humiliation in front of others, an insult, a beating, a kick, sending the child in isolation, locking the child inside a room, not providing food and even not talking to that child for a period of time.

Such a re-course of punishment is not the way to nurture a child, the child one LOVES, our own child.

As a human rights clause the author was expecting UNHRD to say – **"NO PENAL CHARGE ON ANY HUMAN BEING"** in **bold**, CAPITAL and "inverted commas"

The UNHRD falls short on this front.

By recognizing penal as last recourse when a person is proved guilty – even there – UNHRD is suggesting a course of action (paradoxically to its role and purpose) that states: take revenge on a person whom the society might have played a role in making the person criminal who was not criminal in the first place when born.

Some exemptions are given to cases where children are born with mentally different abilities that are not conducive for so called normal society we live in. But there too it is not the fault of the child born with such deficiencies that we define as deficiencies.

In other cases where the child is born normal and grows up to be a criminal why punish a person and not the society that has made possible for the child into becoming a criminal.

The author recommends that one should not agree that UNHRD even recognizes punishment as recourse.

Punishing anyone as a crime is simply idiotic. It is not a *"just system"*; it is protecting a majority, a crowd - a herd mentality.

Punishing someone and sending them to a prison or killing them is in itself a human rights violation. Do people send a sick person to a prison or kill them? Similarly we should expect the UNHRD to look into the humaneness beyond the glasses of law, lawyers, legality, constitution, rule of law.

Such view is what is expected from UNHRD.

The curative place for a person who the society thinks does not fit into their mold of life should be sent to reform school and not to prison, a school that doubles up as a psychological counseling and rehabilitation centre.

Instead of giving a person sympathy and care – those who drafted UNHRD and those bureaucrats who ratified UNHRD have found an easy way out to eliminate criminals and indulge in human rights violations.

The best historic example of this was undertaken by British Empire by establishing a whole country of expelled convicts and criminals between 1788 to 1968 – (The history case of Settlements in Australia, fortunately it ended in 1968)

43. Law and Legal

*T*his might sound repetitive but it is important to repeat because we are trying to understand human rights. If it was another subject like exclusively pertaining to legal laws, the discourse would have been different.

LAW means the system of rules which a particular country or community recognizes as regulating the actions of its members who do not comply with what is written as right; and which it may be enforced by the imposition of penalties.

Law from human rights perspective is in some cases legalizing a crime committed by the state, nation or country; because most laws are always against one or some members of their own society.

Recognizing a penal law within a society is always unjust to a person.

It is taking nature in one's hand and punishing someone – even to the extent of taking a human being's life.

Who are we humans to punish someone?

Recognizing the word punishment and penal as part of the human rights discourse is in itself against human rights.

Laws are made to protect crowds and not for distributing justice to individuals as per whims and fancies of so called intellectuals who term themselves fit to enact penal laws.

Most of the time, law is a tool used to reduce the basic human rights and freedom of an individual and the possibilities of that person to be free to do what one wants to do and be one's own self.

What is required in looking at human rights law are not judges and lawyers but those who understand human nature, human motivations, human psychology and the germination and root causes of crime and violence.

Someone who understands that how wars are continuing from centuries and centuries and the root is the human mind and how the minds take that form of economic and social exploitations resulting in violating human rights. **We require those types of people who can understand and reform the society rather than punish an individual.**

In today's time, if you really understand things intelligently the person who is awarding the punishment as prescribed by law – is more guilty of human rights violation and crimes, but they are legally authorized by constitution and majority and thus not seen as crime under law of the land.

For human rights to work in a healthy environment – there is role of judges and law experts to look into human rights violation is limited because they may not see anything beyond the prism of law and legal – everything resulting in penal and punishment. Their prism starts and ends with punish the criminal.

The UNHRD is not even trying to prevent and / or make people aware to find a cure of the existing half-cooked justice system.

Rather the state in its existing legal processes and justice systems perpetuates and becomes human rights violators.

We should aim for an evolved society where people understand things that law and legal cannot see and find solution of human rights violation, rather it is the interwoven fabric of a cohesive and peaceful communities that handle social well-beings of individuals.

44. Interference

*I*nterference means to interfere into someone's life without invitation; that is what a law against interference is about protecting someone's privacy.

In context of human rights though the clause was included for restricting state interfering into the private lives of their citizen based on the German Nazi's surveillance on their citizen during World War 2.

But today this UNHRD clause applies to anyone who interferes into other's lives without permission.

Applicability of interference with respect to state sounds right – because it would apply to a certain extent to everyone in the society. While on the other hand, those defining *interference* need to see it in context with different and varied world cultures.

In western societies where isolated and lonely adults are psychologically tuned to a BIG ego and 'I' – they fail to have a strong sense of communities, societies entrenched in tradition and families where a group is above an individual and individual exists less than the whole.

To introduce a concept of such interference at individual level on all the cultures of the world would lead to chaos – total chaos and break the spine of thousand years of evolving culture with one stroke of human right awareness of interference.

When applicable to individuals, some ignorant ones may misuse this clause even to consider a helping hand, a social compliment, an extending hand, a loving care as *interference*.

No one wants a debauch society that misuses interference as mentioned in the above paragraph, where the rights of psychotic people are protected by wrong interpretation of this clause and those who are innocent are punished for showing humanity and love towards others.

If the ones who understand human rights law do not see this evident difference of its applicability they would be very poor practitioner of human rights law in reality.

45. Movement

The UNHRD has two clauses that state:

1. Everyone has right to movement and residence within borders of each state
2. Everyone has right to leave any country and return to country

The world is one, and people have drawn a line on Earth to define territories as nations and countries and got affiliations to it through citizenship of being born there or after a required constitutional law and legal process.

Once a person recognizes the existence of borders – the whole issue of human rights with respect to '*movement*' fails.

If UNHRD had defined movement across different borders as a right it would have been correct, but UNHRD does not offer that solution. It states movement within states and thus inherently recognizes the borders. It is a very narrow way of destroying the concept of "**World-without-borders**"

Recognition of borders in itself is a violation of human rights that UNHRD is committing and abusing its role as holder of human rights flag.

The UNHRD only talks about everyone have a right to leave and return to country.

Why not make earth and the world as a single place where movement is free?

This clause of **movement** looks is a BIG conspiracy or a short-sightedness while drafting the UNHRD.

UN and the UNHRD - both are becoming partners in violating and endorsing the restrictive movements of individuals based on the inbuilt assumptions of terms and conditions and legal laws of each land.

The power of violating the human rights is given legitimately under the UNHRD to the states and declaration does not step into defending the human rights of people who are migrants and who travel from one region to another due to natural or man-made calamities – like famine and/or war.

It is such a shame and ugly to continue carry on this "freedom to movement" declaration in its current wordings within the UNHRD.

This is the most obnoxious and a regressive clause within UNHRD.

With the current understanding of movements it becomes extremely difficult to impose any war crime case against a single nation or country except *appealing* to them for permitting refugees to stay within and migrants to cross borders without obeying certain dictums and laws of the land.

The UNHRD is best used when it is an instrument against the law of the land, but in this case – the UNHRD inherently accepts and endorses just the opposite of the conceptual and fundamental meaning of movement should be.

Despiteful!

46. Asylum

Asylum in human rights terminology is generally believed to be understood as a place where someone seeks protection.

The UNHRD principle says that every human being has a right to seek asylum.

The **caveat** here is that people who seek asylum cannot do so if they have done something against the purpose and principles of UN. (refer to Principles of UNHRD in Chapter 4)

Let us understand who can seek asylum?

Those who fear for their lives can and may seek asylum to another country.

What happens in case of a massive war where millions of people migrate and want to seek asylum with other countries? Is it possible and acceptable by other countries who do not want to open their borders to integrate migrants within their population?

What role UN plays to making a comfortable route and refuge to asylum seekers?

It is nice to write idealistic things but under UNHRD it is impossible to implement with non-existent implementing procedures within any nation states, except mild diplomatic dialogue expecting some compliance.

Individual asylum seeking may be possible (though one has to go through the rigors of visa process and bureaucratic and political systems), but mass asylum pressure on any country is seen to be a difficult proposition – next to impossible.

Until there are national borders and the UN assumes the recognition of such borders - the UNHRD will remain mere words and a platform – or a club to debate and argue.

Forwarding the earlier chapter's argument here – that by assuming certain existing scenario that does not allow nation to implement UNHRD - and UN recognizing those failures; by this way UN becomes partners in crime in human rights violation and abuse, because it does not and cannot offer any solution nor is it in a position to do so.

47. Self-Determination

Self Determination is broadly defined as people determine their own laws, legislation and how people want to be governed and live as members of their own group, state, nation, region etc.

Self-determination is a bit complicated concept than it seems by its wordings thus it is a bit difficult one to dissect.

Since childhood there is no free-will of individuals because parents, family, community, social circles influence and make the majority of decision making of/ for an individual, so in that context there is nothing like self-determination when one is programmed from childhood in certain ways of thinking, behavior and attitudes.

Self-determination in its truest sense does not exist.

Self-determination majorly should be seen as a family and societal decision on self-determination (as group or majority decision) in most parts of the world because not a single individual grows and lives in isolation.

And the same logic applies from family, to community to state and nation.

48. Persecution

*P*ersecution is defined as hostility and ill-treatment and punishment under law or by majority population with support from the ruling state because of someone's race, ethnicity, color, political, religious beliefs, speaking against government, or in recent cases because of association with human rights activism activities, human rights defenders,

When a particular community feels prosecuted because of any of the above factors, the community and its members can seek asylum in other country.

In certain cases, a fanatic state and governing dictatorship may prosecute members of their state just for criticizing the way things happen within their society and state. This type of persecution though based on minor criticism is a sign of increasing human rights violations within the state.

Does criticism of governance contribute to persecution of any kind? What role UN plays when such cases are there and the local rule of law does not protect the rights of people nor there is a case made to UN for asylum? How is the protection granted to those individuals or group?

These are some of the un-answered questions.

49. Nationality

Nationality is of an individual and / or of group belonging to a nation. Sometimes it is also referred as **nationhood.**

The concept of nation and nationhood pertain to sharing a political, religious, regional identity for self-determination as a nation-state.

At one level of understanding Nationality is not a unifying force. It is a divisive concept that divides humans with boundaries and nationalities that further their individualistic fervor of nationhood to compete with other nations.

Sadly, Nationalism is a feeling of superiority of one's nation over other. It becomes a root cause of human rights violations. **This is also a sure seed of possible human rights violation in future.**

One of the factors that contribute to increasing trend of human rights violation is this affiliation to nationality and the things that go around in protecting national pride.

Let us look at another word closely confused with nationalism – **Patriotism.**

Patriotism is the inner factor of Nationality. Patriotism is devotion and support for one's country's values and culture.

Both qualities – Nationalism and Patriotism may seem appealing to common person of a nation, but in broader context if not understood properly both may lead to subjecting other citizens and humans to human rights violations.

Now let us come to the clause on Nationality in UNHRD. **"No one shall be arbitrarily deprived of one's nationality or denied the right to change one's nationality"**

Here the catch phrase is arbitrarily one cannot deprive any person of one's nationality but with proper reasons one can. **Then this too should be considered as a human rights violation.**

If one has to change one's nationality it is like going from one pit to another pit of degrading philosophy about this nation is better than that nation; a process that need not be recognized at all in the human rights context.

Do remember that we are talking here philosophically and not those cases where people seek other nationality because their current nationality is suffocating them.

It is always under the umbrella of nationalism and patriotism – internal and external to one's nations - human rights violations happen without any consequences of guilt.

The moment a person belongs to a nation, and when a person realizes this nationalism and its affiliations, slowly with time that person's patriotism takes birth and chances are that the seeds of human violations are also sown along with this realization.

Thus ideally human rights abuse and violation is minimum when it is over and above such terms as nationalism and patriotism, and these terms need not be part of any UNHRD.

50. Marriage

The UNHRD clearly defines some clauses for men and women and their relationship. Of course, we are talking of **marriage** here.

The author wonders why the experts of the drafting committee have jumped a few initial encounters between men and women or girl and a boy and directly talking of marriage and its human rights implications.

Strange over-look!

We will come back to that later. Let us understand in simple terms what does it say?

- Man and woman have right to marry and have a family
- Marriage is something that is entered with free and full consent of man and woman
- Family is natural group of society and should be protected by the state

Now this looks quite simple to read from the outset.

UNHRD does not go beyond the superficial definition of **marriage - as an institution which is legally and formally recognized by some jurisdiction of law, religion and culture.**

Author would like to say here that to enter a bond between man and woman with a form of contract – that in itself is a human right violation of one individual's trust, faith, love and dignity.

One of the two spouses in a marriage contract may feel offended for the breach of their trust both have right at the beginning of the alliance. Their personal trust (if any) on being together is now being replaced by a piece of paper and a contractual obligation over-seen by a society, community or legislation.

Sensitive human beings would look at the whole process of marriage as a violation of the inherent goodness a person carries in heart for another person.

"Why we need to get married, don't you trust me?"

On the same lines, taking one step before any marriage, why does not UNHRD also clearly say that about other genders apart from man and woman and other forms of alliance that are solely based on respect, trust and love.

Why UNHRD does not protected those too? Like, for example:

- Men and women of any other or same gender have a right to LOVE each other
- Men and women of any other or same gender have a right to live together with or without formal contract or ratification of any jurisdiction – legal or social.

Here is where the UNHRD falls short in its liberal outlook in restricting its preview only to marriage and no other love alliances between human beings.

51. Property

*P*roperty means a thing or things possessed by an individual or by a group of people.

Under human rights law property may mostly mean land or a building called as property.

Through centuries, property is the sole reason of dispute resulting in human rights violations.

To formulate a law under human rights is a non-sustainable form of looking at our planet.

This is a typical European view of buying land under a fabricated law and contract – **a land which does even belong to human beings in the first place**. Humans have self-nominated themselves as guardian of the earth, planet and nature and destroyed everything on this planet with this attitude.

In that process people with such attitudes have constructed laws to fool everyone about their rights on the planet earth – so that every exploitations is done in the name of development in the form of legal sanction.

History has many example of how land is illegally occupied by explorers and invaders and called it their land – this logic extends from a small piece of land to a whole continent (Australia, New Zealand and North America and Latin America)

That is why the Indian American could never understand the whole proposition of European invaders coming to their land and offering them a price to buy the land.

The inclusion of Property as a valid clause in UNHRD is giving sanctity and legality to allow people to occupy land through means – often legal.

But in actuality all this are illegal ways to exploit nature, environment and ecology.

The declaration states that *"Everyone has a right to own property and no one shall be arbitrarily deprived of a property."*

If one is strictly talking of land, then **land is limited resource on the planet earth** and those with wealth and money can buy ample amount of land legally leaving the majority of population landless But after a point – from where anyone is going to supplement land – when all land is purchased by someone or the other.

Under UNHRD law all property deals are justified as it is every person's *right* to buy property. So a wrong is justified by a *right* under UNHRD – the right of exploiting limited resources gets legal sanction under UNHRD. **A little bit of common sense tells us that such a thing is great human environmental calamity, if not for now – for the future of humanity, planet earth and ecology.**

This clause is where the UNHRD falls hugely short of protecting the planet earth and human rights of poor people, especially aboriginals.

52. Arbitrary

These word 'arbitrary' figures in the UNHRD often, at least four times as – **arbitrary** *arrest*, **arbitrary** *interference*, **arbitrarily** *deprived of nationality* and **arbitrarily** *deprived of property*, so it is impertinent to understand what is arbitrary, and how does that work in real life.

Arbitrary means - based and subject to a person's whims, prejudices and fancies.

Each and every decision one person or a group of people take is in some way arbitrary, because it is loaded with personal beliefs, groundings and social learning which may never be objective to the person for whom the decision is made, because they may not have lived the person's life for a single second.

Most decisions making processes, the way it happens is based on a discussion, debates, arguments by the most logical, rational and intelligent person in the room, who can present and articulate and convince others.

But there is no reason to believe that logic, intelligence and rationality will always lead to fair and humane decisions that will surely hold upright the human rights of a person.

The person or a group who is in the 'power' and authority gets the last word and that itself is so arbitrary.

Take the case of Democratic voting process that takes place, where the all aspects and outcomes are discussed– especially the benefits and losses that the immediate group will face due to their casting of a certain vote.

But the biases and prejudices are loaded during the build up to the democratic voting – not leaving any persons to be fair and un-biased or non-prejudiced during voting and leading to the process of voting.

Thus to consider and assume that a person or a group will be fair and not influenced by the current electorate climate - political, economic and social structures and media pressures is totally false.

In this world there is nothing like "**not arbitrary**".

Most and all decision a person makes are arbitrary to a certain extend because a decision in itself is a power loaded tool equipped with complex factors that breed within a mind and those factors can never be discounted.

53. Thought

*A*re we free to think?

We may say YES, but think carefully – since childhood we are programmed by our parents, family, friends, relatives, community, school, teachers and leaders to believe in the words they say, show and make us read that impresses our tender minds.

Here we are not talking of the right or wrong content of that initial programming of our mind. Many traditional and modern cultures teach children things that are picked up unconsciously and a human life is lived believing that to be true.

Thought is a very deceptive tool within human body.

So when someone talks of Freedom of thought, there is no real freedom of thought except those who are aware of the mind-games thought plays on them and others.

Those who can be aware of such things – are mostly out-classed and boycotted for not adhering themselves to the herd-mentality of the majority.

So Freedom of Thought as mentioned in the UNHRD is a "NO-NO" beginner in the first place.

54. Conscience

Conscience is your moral learning since childhood.

It is created inside humans by the society we live in. A Christian conscience is different from Muslim conscience to a Buddhist conscience to any other conscience of a culture, tradition, religion and region.

Thus conscience is not same - it is different for different person.

The fact remains that most people believe that their conscience is better than the others. This leads one conscience to be abusive of other conscience.

Then what is the use of conscience, when recognition of conscience can lead to some exploitation and abuse?

Conscience is inculcated in humans in a schizophrenic way. It divides humans in different moralities, and thus it is abusive of humanity because it has the seeds of creating conflicts between humans.

Conscience not only allows one human group to dominate other group but also makes the group being dominated believe that they exist to be enslaved to the other groups of so called intellectuals – such as priests and politicians and policy makers.

When one aligns oneself with a moral value and virtue – one is forced to do something in obligation and / or guilt to comply with the society one lives in – this is conscience.

One who understands the origin and realities of the way conscience works in real life – **it is the meanest thing to be invented by mind to create division, divisiveness and havoc to human society.**

Conscience is a very subtle method of slavery of the mind.

Mind is never free to decide anything on its own; it is bond by conscience that is dictated by something higher that one has learned in childhood as right or wrong. It becomes artificial.

When the consciences works there is an inner feeling of someone is watching you and you should not be doing certain things.

People obeying and following conscience look stupid because they are not using their own sense of life and living experience It is borrowed from someone's learning about life and thus it is static.

Once conscience is ingrained in as a child, the child carries the burden of that conscience (right or wrong) till one dies.

Living by conscience makes human live in guilt forever.

Humans should live with freedom not with guilt.

Where is freedom of conscience?

The UNHRD has got the whole definition and understanding of conscience wrong.

The need is to drop conscience entirely from UNHRD. It is necessity, be free from it and no one should have freedom to chose conscience, but one should be aware and build consciousness and not live in and by one's *'cage of conscience'*.

55. *Religion*

Religion is another divisive concept and should not have any place in the human rights narrative.

Religion creates division of humanity, affiliations and human mind further creates through religion feelings of better and worse. This gives rise to abuse, power and comparison – everything negative.

In today's fanatic times - religion is an institution that enslaves people to follow certain dictum as per their norms, and there is no freedom in following a restrictive path. A path that leads nowhere - except abuse deriving out of the power of knowing the religious truth by priest and holy person.

Those who wrote the declarations do not understand that by giving religion a place is giving place to intolerance and human rights abuse in the declaration.

Religion in its own is something a person, only a person can believe in.

The moment there are two people agreeing on religion it becomes politics! Politics of any kind should not find a place in UNHRD.

The real religion is like science ever evolving but the scripture of each religion has made it an inorganic and stale text.

In today's world we have seen that the word Religion is creating wars and strategic expansion of religious faith through lures and incentives. Such things exist and thus religion as a concept should be kept out of UNHRD.

Why include religion when it is surely going to lead the world to disastrous catastrophe?

Let UNHRD be positive and avoid such pitfalls.

Practicing religion inside one's heart, worship, pray, belief, practice and observe oneself is what is required; but not as a couple, not in a group, not as a society, not as a religious cult. This is disastrous for humanity and human rights.

Religion is an individual faith and belief and it should be like that. But instead religion has now become a business and should be left out of the UNHRD.

56. Opinion and Expressions

When one speaks one is expressing an opinion.

What is an opinion?

It is a judgment about something based on certain knowledge – it may be right or wrong.

Just because one has got the ability to speak or write one ventures into this terrain of expressing. It is absolutely impossible to be certain about attaining all the knowledge before one speaks. Thus anyone speaking may not be existing reality or certainly the *'truth'*.

Such opinions and expressions may result in creating discord within humanity and between human beings, individuals, groups, societies, cultures, nations and ethnicity.

By recognizing the right to speak anything - not only UNHRD gives the right to create discord within society, it actually helps to create an atmosphere of human rights violations and abuse.

That is what is happening in today's world. There are arguments, debates, opinions, expressions about each and everything. Internet and social media platforms give free access to speak any nonsense and get away with it.

If there is a position, you will always find a group with counter position and humans fighting tooth and nail defending a position that is believed to be true by both opposite views and parties fighting.

In any case the one that has power, money, wealth or the one who has number of people to indulge in violence will try its best to win the argument or difference of opinion.

Mostly opinions are majority accepted, so the views of minority groups are always curtailed. UNHRD does not address that process.

If freedom of speech is going to harm people and abuse their rights they are a useless freedom of speech.

Freedom of speech resulting in humiliation and insults can result in life-long harm, suicide and curtailing a human life – that too is a human rights abuse.

Freedom of speech that hurts and provokes another person to indulge in an act of violence should be curtailed in UNHRD.

We want to live in a peaceful society – that is the purpose and not in a society where everyone is spiteful of others.

The opinions starting with ideas and discussed as ideas should be the only thing permissible within UNHRD.

The moment it crosses that boundary beyond one's idea and trespasses respect of another human being

– it becomes a political instrument to pave way for human rights abuses of one group dominating over others in some way or the other – through words, writing, policies, dictates or even actions that result from an extreme opinion and expression.

57. Assembly and Association

Assembly is a group of people meeting for a common purpose.

Unlike many other places "a peaceful assembly" is the one adjective that is added to define assembly that is considered good under UNHRD.

Similarly UNHRD can do the same with freedom of speech that does not harm or hurt anyone, or does not humiliate and insult others.

Association too is very similar meaning like assembly – simply meaning **a group of people organized for a joint purpose.**

The difference in definition is that in assembly they meet and in association they organize.

After forming an association, one can have an assembly and association as a body and entity.

The UNHRD says that no one should be compelled to become member of an association.

Here the important word to understand is '*compelled*'.

Compel means force and oblige.

Any human act that forces and obliges another human to do something - that **act** is always against human rights and should be considered as violation of human will.

The author would like to list down words that one should remember that fall into the same category. This is required to avoid any human rights abuse from your side – try to be aware to not do any acts that could be understood as any of the follows:

> *Compel, force, coerce, oblige, press, enforce, impress, exact, subjugate, command, persuade, convince, induce, impel, push, power, thrust, ram, drive, pressure and many other words and...*

...their variants that fall into unnecessary forcing someone to do certain things in any way.

58. *Government*

Government means a group of people who are given authority to govern over others.

Govern means conduct the policy, affairs and actions with authority.

As we have understood earlier, that power is a corrupting and leading factor to human rights abuse.

If that is the case, *why one should give someone power to rule over them with authority. Is not that an issue giving rise to human rights abuses?*

Basically in selecting government the general population is stating that we believe in a person or a group with certain values and ideology to rule over us. We have chosen a group to rule over us.

This scenario is delicate - because people have chosen a group to govern them, even if government indulges in human rights abuses the group can always turn back and say – *"You appointed us, next election do not elect us"* and get immunity for their crimes.

To understand government in much more philosophical way is to understand that good government is actually NO PRESENCE OF GOVERNMENT.

People have been brainwashed to believe in democracy and fooled to believe that they are electing someone to rule over them through government systems and processes.

If you meet and talk to a few officers and ministers of the government, you will know what a grave mistake you have made through a process called democracy to make this idiots rule over you. There are ample examples of such democratically elected people who are stupid and foolish.

The problem is people who know things are not ready to take the burden and responsibility of governance, and people who do not know take this responsibility - not for the sake of governance, but to make money and attain power over others.

People who are elected are mostly power hungry people. They really do not want to govern, the want to be in power, because with power they can get wealth, fame, popularity and domination to do what they want to do.

The above ideation is a very dangerous phenomenon of and for democracy.

There are instances of where an Education Minister (appointed democratically by people) is an illiterate. Not only that the Minister indulges in a criminal act of procuring a false & fake education certificate. It is hilarious and astonishing too!

This is what democracy and government can deliver if people are not aware of such dangers.

Democracy does not work when majority of people are ignorant and kept that way due to lack of rightful information and education.

Other phenomenon of Government is that people almost worship the one whom they elect and are unable to see any flaws objectively.

Things are changing with the emergence of new media and internet where information reaches people so much and so fast that no one is to check the trueness of that information and authenticity of what people digest in their minds.

But here too the social media, electronic and print media are used to propagate fake news to sway wrong impression and create fear-psychosis for or against a particular individual or group of people.

Government is a power centre and it is bound to abuse human rights in some way – even if it does not try to do that intentionally.

People should be educated and made aware of merits of a person who is there to serve and not to govern.

Government is a euphemism used to believe they are serving masses and population – but it actually means they are in power ruling over the population.

How about **"Servement"** *instead of Government?*

Some intellectual may argue that civilization may not survive without a government. Actually these intellectuals are fooling you with their ignorance because they have never gone beyond thinking outside their little gray-box.

150

Government is basically a system where a few humans get to call themselves government for short while and this group of people irrespective of their merit or caliber get power and authority to decide what is good for everyone, meaning treat everyone around like slaves.

If these small groups of people are a crazy lot they can even commit mass murders, they can do it legally by declaring war within or outside their state boundaries and give it a name of patriotic and nationalism to the violence and human rights abuses they commit through it.

These people who are selected or elected get the sanction to sign, prepare, use and abuse power, money and rob public deposits and get inside information to become rich through *'policy mandated wealth benefits'* accruing through upcoming projects and property.

All Government in the end works as a corrupt system, evil, lying, stealing, committing human rights abuses.

Knowing the way actual governments run - Government as a word should not be even figure in the UNHRD.

59. Public Service

*P*ublic Service is anything provided by the system governing the population (*here* government) for the people, and everyone has equal right meaning access to these public services.

For the sake of convenience let us list down the public services:

- Electricity

- Education (e.g. state public schools, public universities)

- Emergency services (e.g. Fire, Law Enforcement, Search and Rescue, Disaster Relief etc...)

- Environmental protection

- Gas and oil

- Health care

- Military

- Postal service

- Public bank

- Public broadcasting

- Public library

- Public security

- Public transportation

- Social services, (e.g. public housing, social welfare, food subsidies, etc...)

- Telecommunications

- Urban planning

- Transportation infrastructure

- Waste management (e.g. wastewater, solid waste, recycling, etc...)

- Water supply network

Not to say that in reality these things exists. In poor and developing countries the rich get access and poor still live without basic public services making the whole public service system an instrument of human rights abuses.

60. Democracy & Elections

One clause of UNHRD talks about **Elections - to choose a person by voting – a person who can govern all people. That is what is called process of** *democracy.*

We have discussed parts of this earlier in the chapter of Government.

People elect their representatives, whom we called politicians, and all of us know what politics mean, and who politicians are, and what they do after getting elected?

Though they are given the power to govern and rule over us, but in reality majority of them are there to make money, have power, loot people, benefit their kin and community, rob public money so on and so forth.

That is what we call the system of democracy, where outwardly everyone seems to be happy – that masses are given importance to take part in the election of choosing who will be their ruler, under whom they would like to be slave of.

The need is to break this slave mentality. Once you break that – democracy will disappear.

Democracy survives because there are people who want to be enslaved, abused and exploited by those few who govern them, the government, the politicians, the system and the democratic process.

When democracy is the foundation of human rights abuse should UNHRD propagate it as an instrument to human rights savior?

The way democracy is practiced should end to bring an end to human rights abuses.

For that elections should go away. Those who are fooled to think they are given "*a power*" to elect a person to rule over them, those people should be educated about the devastation this system has brought.

This system of democracy through election looks innocent, but it is not.

Democracy is a "**mobocracy**" that makes people frenzied, it perpetuates the herd-mentality, what one is doing, everyone else does, where is the wind blowing everyone blindly follows it.

Of course in historical evolution of societies, democracy is better than dictatorship, but looking into reality and its drawbacks and track-record of the number of human rights abuses take place under this system of democracy, it should be kept out of UNHRD.

Under the mask of democracy every bad thing is permissible under law. There is very little done for poor, but it is showed much more is done for poor.

Democracy brings forth a dictator (*of varying degrees***) elected by people.**

Democracy will still survive for centuries till majority of populace awaken, and then one day democracy will fall, because it is a corrupt system against ignorant humanity.

61. *Work*

Work is an activity that may involve mental and physical effort to achieve a result.

As per UNHRD everyone has a choice to work whatever they want and wherever they want.

The question is what if a person on their own free choice – choose to work as a slave in one's ignorance or even being aware of it due to circumstances one is fated in?

Why one would intentionally work as a slave?

If the current economy will give rise to unemployment and no job opportunities are there for people to earn a comfortable livelihood – thus people are forced to do work; select work below their dignity, caliber, qualifications and feel humiliated, insulted just like a slave.

Though everything seems hunky dory, this is the case and scenario in most parts of the world.

People are free to choose to work but their choices are forced on them, because they have to survive, live and earn a livelihood.

UNHRD does not talk about this fact that no human being could be forced to work below his qualification, experience and caliber just for a livelihood and living.

Such types of incidents also should be considered as a human rights abuses existing in the society that needs to be avoided.

UNHRD overlooks this factor and talks about equal pay for equal work, but does not talk about under-utilized talent pool exploitation as human rights violation.

Rather the modern society mostly puts the onus of blame on the human being as an unmotivated individual and subjects the person to further de-humanizing treatment for inability to find and do work.

62. Rest Leisure & Work

The UNHRD defines that **everyone should have a reasonable limit of rest and leisure during work in terms of number of hours and holidays.**

The issues of human rights come into picture where the work conditions are deplorable as in informal and unregulated sectors.

Here the government does not have control and monitoring over the enterprises that employ local people with under-wage and over-time.

Within informal sector, where the entrepreneur is himself the owner and worker – there could be a permissible allowance of leverage given to how many extra hours one works.

But when an owner of a small or medium enterprise employs someone – sometimes, young children (are made to work illegally) below permissible age, under-pays them, over-works them, in unhygienic conditions with no leisure time and rest – causes concerns for human rights violation and abuse.

We see that lots of UNHRD clauses assumes and accept a system that is corrupt and tries to put a human rights clause to prevent it.

The case in point here is when profit is the driving motive – there is no way one can stop exploitation and human rights violations or environmental degradation.

The equation is simple: pay out as little as possible in rent, wages, services and gain out maximum in terms of profit margin from consumers. That is profit!

The author has a problem with such assumption, because recognizing an existing system that is inefficiently exploitative, de-meaning and abusive need not be covered under UNHRD.

By doing that one is giving legitimization to a corrupt system within human civilization.

Market system has failed miserably in benefiting all.

Thought there are people who say that some people becoming rich will lead to the majority being rich and coming out of the poverty circle, but history has shown otherwise. **The richer have become richer and poor poorer.**

The world was duped by these concepts of open-market-economy, globalization and even by communist and socialist ideologies.

Work is shifted from developed countries to developing countries where there are no laws to protect workers, where wages are low, and the working conditions are compromised.

The question to ask is – whether UNHRD need to acknowledge any work system that could be exploitative – should UNHRD also give a warning against those systems?

The author recommends that UNHRD should define and warn against abusive systems!

63. Social Protection

Social protection consists of a package of policies and programs floated by the elected government to provide security of food, education, water, electricity, shelter, health to their citizens.

There are some sectors where government plays a key role in delivery of security and social protection to those who are needy, poor and require special treatment.

By not providing this type of social protection the result may be human rights violations of their citizens.

The problem with social protection and security is that the society is disintegrating its ethos, tradition and culture under the new emerging system of centralized government public service delivery.

For example, the cleanliness of common areas done by the local community leaders in many places in the world about a century ago – is neglected by the new millennia generation who grow up knowing it is government's job to clean the common areas. So the new generation does not take an initiative to clean up nor does government perform its role to clean up. **In the end, it is a dirty surrounding and environment that people and communities live in.**

The security and social protection extended by the government are in some ways killing the societal fabric that existed from thousands of years where local communities took personal and community responsibilities to maintain basic social protection and services in their purview.

The same case is true for water and forest conservation which was the prerogative and of interest to local community in rural communities and villages; now they are not doing anything because everyone thinks – it is government's role to provide water and protect forests.

Thus people have stopped conserving water and also protecting the traditional forests and animals which that were guarded and worshipped.

These are the big drawbacks of providing social protection and security by any central system and authority.

The government and state should not snatch away the existing practices that are on-going and replace them with a centralized and corrupt system that does not work, leaving the citizen's in lurch of basic services and amenities.

There are some common services like sustainable light, emergency, health services and sanitation that government can provide through quality accessible services packages.

Accessibility is the key issue in delivery of quality social protection and security services mentioned above especially health, specialized health services, education and professional education colleges.

The point one is making here is: By including the mandate of social protection on government or state to provide basic human rights protection – the mandate is invariantly breaking away the existing human rights protection that prevailed through culture and traditions from thousands of years.

Not does Government is able to deliver on its promises nor the community takes initiatives to maintain the status quo the way before it became government's mandate.

The overall cost-benefit analysis of the above give and take roles and mandates between government and community responsibilities has in the end resulted in more people denied of their basic human rights services, and are forced to live in a sub-standard environment and surroundings like slums and settlements.

64. Culture

*W*hen we talk of Culture and human rights it is very important to understand from where "*Culture*" word came into being within UNHRD.

Briefly, it was during the late twentieth century – in the early nineteen nineties to be precise - the dissolution and fall of Soviet Union happened where about 15 countries under the former Soviet Union of Russia - the communist regime - had over-powered local cultures under the hammer of government laws and bureaucracy.

This clause under UNHRD was to give the new formed countries of Soviet Russia confidence to carry on with their local cultures, arts, religion, life, literary, artistic history.

Thus it is worth reading the article of UNHRD on culture with that perspective in mind – though narrowly written, it is applicable universally.

The caution here is the existence of law that undermines local culture for the benefit of nation and patriotic ideals. That too has the potential of curtailing of community culture that they have traditionally followed historically in their families and communities.

Any system – communist, market driven, nationalist, and socialist and many more have the same fear and danger to curtailing rights of freely participating in culture and social life.

65. Copyright

Copyright *rights* are another right that is included in the UNHRD.

Copyright gives exclusive and legal rights to – print, publish, perform, film, literary, artistic, music, scientific productions.

Copyright has a short history. The oldest reference of copyright talk is referred to 1710 AD in Britain when books were **not** allowed to be copied without permission of the law.

The motivation of drafting copyright laws was always based on profit-motive and making money for the inventor and creator for the creative input, resources and time spent.

Before this British copyright law of 1710 A.D. anything human beings did was for the benefit of the society. All knowledge was free to share; all knowledge was for everyone and it was not with a thought of gaining wealth. That was the welfare spirit with no selfish gain for oneself.

This root thought of making money and profit out of an invention was first implemented by Britain and spread to European and then to United States – later it was internationalized to every country in the world.

The question to ask here is:

Is copyright law ethical for common good?

There are millions of instances and cases all over the world where new creations and inventions have been kept at bay from reaching out to all the people (especially poor) because of the copyright laws.

Copyright law is only benefitting those who can pay a price to avail its benefit; one has money to buy a part of the production.

Copyright laws discriminates poor and poverty.

The great balancer to copyright law has come in this is the invention of internet and all copyright material – especially for written, published, literary, audio, videos, software and so much more – which (though) illegally provides free access to all the things that people are interested in.

Though all these comes under the illegal framework of current international copy right laws but works as a great balancer.

There is a school of thought that says that nothing in this world should come into the "copyright law" making the UNHRD clause – nil and void.

This UNHRD copyright clause does not consider the fact of an open, transparent, emerging and evolving young society – where any government control over anything is seen with despise because now intelligent people who are aware understand that such protection to copyright laws is a real exploiter in benefitting the rich and violating the poor's right to live.

This is another instance where UNHRD supports copyright laws by mentioning it in its clauses, and restricts the far reaching benefits to the most poor.

The whole act of non-reach is in itself a human rights violation for many especially when the copyrighted invention is medical and health related.

66. International Order

The drafting of the clause on "social and international order" seen in the UNHRD is a dichotomy and paradoxical entitlement of rights.

Here under UNHRD the purpose of International order is focused more on building an international trade and it is related to money, and wealth.

Social order on other hand is a personal issue to build the character of a person.

On one side UNHRD talks about right for a social order, and on other side it also talks of the other spectrum – international order.

One needs to understand that recognizing an **international order is a power hierarchy thing**. It is not a soft issue like social order which is unique from place to place, region to region, society to society, family to family.

In one breathe one cannot put both together. There are many treaties on the evolutionary process of combining these two rights together, but it seems hotchpotch combination – that does not make sense.

67. *Subject To*

*T*he one clause of UNHRD nullifies all the other human rights clauses by putting in a word "subject to…"

When "*Subject to*" is mentioned whenever and wherever in UNHRD it means **rights are given subject to the local existing laws.**

It is like saying we at UN do not take responsibility of anything written under UNHRD if it is not equivocally supported by local government and legal system to maintain just requirement of morality, public order and general welfare.

This clause and "subject to" is utterly disappointing for the whole humanity.

It is a BIG letdown of UNHRD. It shows UN and its ratified drafts like UNHRD are only like paper tigers.

It is like saying "*You are right but…*"; which should be understood as that anything that precedes **"but"** is a lie. And "*subject to*" fits same in that bill of "*but*" – it tells that everything written till now in the UNHRD is a lie.

68. The Last Clause

The last clause of UNHRD pleads and begs to declare that please do not interpret or try to imply any of the words, clauses in this UNHRD that is aimed at destruction of any rights and freedom.

Basically it says that please do not write such / any books to actually explain the meaning of UNHRD in simple terms that could be understood by all.

The content of this current book falls into that category which exposes the UNHRD drafting committee who wrote with outlaid wrong assumptions and faulty recognition to existing exploitative system that remains abusive even after formulating the UNHRD.

UNHRD AS IT IS

Preamble

Whereas recognition of the inherent dignity and of the equal and inalienable rights of all members of the human family is the foundation of freedom, justice and peace in the world,

Whereas disregard and contempt for human rights have resulted in barbarous acts which have outraged the conscience of mankind, and the advent of a world in which human beings shall enjoy freedom of speech and belief and freedom from fear and want is proclaimed as the highest aspiration of the common people,

Whereas it is essential, if man is not to be compelled to have recourse, as a last resort, to rebellion against tyranny and oppression, that human rights should be protected by the rule of law,

Whereas it is essential to promote the development of friendly relations between nations,

Whereas the peoples of the UN have in the Charter reaffirmed their faith in fundamental human rights, in the dignity and worth of the human person and in the equal rights of men and women and have determined to promote social progress and better standards of life in larger freedom,

Whereas Member States have pledged themselves to achieve, in co-operation with the UN, the promotion of universal respect for and observance of human rights and fundamental freedoms,

Whereas a common understanding of these rights and freedoms is of the greatest importance for the full realization of this pledge,

Now, Therefore THE GENERAL ASSEMBLY proclaims THIS UNIVERSAL DECLARATION OF HUMAN RIGHTS as a common standard of achievement for all peoples and all nations, to the end that every individual and every organ of society, keeping this Declaration constantly in mind, shall strive by teaching and education to promote respect for these rights and freedoms and by progressive measures, national and international, to secure their universal and effective recognition and observance, both among the peoples of Member States themselves and among the peoples of territories under their jurisdiction.

Article 1.

All human beings are born free and equal in dignity and rights. They are endowed with reason and conscience and should act towards one another in a spirit of brotherhood.

Article 2.

Everyone is entitled to all the rights and freedoms set forth in this Declaration, without distinction of any kind, such as race, colour, sex, language, religion, political or other opinion, national or social origin, property, birth or other status. Furthermore, no distinction shall be made on the basis of the political, jurisdictional or international status of the country or territory to which a person belongs, whether it be independent, trust, non-self-governing or under any other limitation of sovereignty.

Article 3.

Everyone has the right to life, liberty and security of person.

Article 4.

No one shall be held in slavery or servitude; slavery and the slave trade shall be prohibited in all their forms.

Article 5.

No one shall be subjected to torture or to cruel, inhuman or degrading treatment or punishment.

Article 6.

Everyone has the right to recognition everywhere as a person before the law.

Article 7.

All are equal before the law and are entitled without any discrimination to equal protection of the law. All are entitled to equal protection against any discrimination in violation of this Declaration and against any incitement to such discrimination.

Article 8.

Everyone has the right to an effective remedy by the competent national tribunals for acts violating the fundamental rights granted him by the constitution or by law.

Article 9.

No one shall be subjected to arbitrary arrest, detention or exile.

Article 10.

Everyone is entitled in full equality to a fair and public hearing by an independent and impartial tribunal, in the determination of his rights and obligations and of any criminal charge against him.

Article 11.

(1) Everyone charged with a penal offence has the right to be presumed innocent until proved guilty according to law in a public trial at which he has had all the guarantees necessary for his defence.

(2) No one shall be held guilty of any penal offence on account of any act or omission which did not constitute a penal offence, under national or international law, at the time when it was committed. Nor shall a heavier penalty be imposed than the one that was applicable at the time the penal offence was committed.

Article 12.

No one shall be subjected to arbitrary interference with his privacy, family, home or correspondence, nor to attacks upon his honour and reputation. Everyone has the right to the protection of the law against such interference or attacks.

Article 13.

(1) Everyone has the right to freedom of movement and residence within the borders of each state.

(2) Everyone has the right to leave any country, including his own, and to return to his country.

Article 14.

(1) Everyone has the right to seek and to enjoy in other countries asylum from persecution.

(2) This right may not be invoked in the case of prosecutions genuinely arising from non-political crimes or from acts contrary to the purposes and principles of the UN.

Article 15.

(1) Everyone has the right to a nationality.

(2) No one shall be arbitrarily deprived of his nationality nor denied the right to change his nationality.

Article 16.

(1) Men and women of full age, without any limitation due to race, nationality or religion, have the right to marry and to found a family. They are entitled to equal rights as to marriage, during marriage and at its dissolution.

(2) Marriage shall be entered into only with the free and full consent of the intending spouses.

(3) The family is the natural and fundamental group unit of society and is entitled to protection by society and the State.

Article 17.

(1) Everyone has the right to own property alone as well as in association with others.

(2) No one shall be arbitrarily deprived of his property.

Article 18.

Everyone has the right to freedom of thought, conscience and religion; this right includes freedom to change his religion or belief, and freedom, either alone or in community with others and in public or private, to manifest his religion or belief in teaching, practice, worship and observance.

Article 19.

Everyone has the right to freedom of opinion and expression; this right includes freedom to hold opinions without interference and to seek, receive and impart information and ideas through any media and regardless of frontiers.

Article 20.

(1) Everyone has the right to freedom of peaceful assembly and association.

(2) No one may be compelled to belong to an association.

Article 21.

(1) Everyone has the right to take part in the government of his country, directly or through freely chosen representatives.

(2) Everyone has the right of equal access to public service in his country.

(3) The will of the people shall be the basis of the authority of government; this will shall be expressed in periodic and genuine elections which shall be by universal and equal suffrage and shall be held by secret vote or by equivalent free voting procedures.

Article 22.

Everyone, as a member of society, has the right to social security and is entitled to realization, through national effort and international co-operation and in accordance with the organization and resources of each State, of the economic, social and cultural rights indispensable for his dignity and the free development of his personality.

Article 23.

(1) Everyone has the right to work, to free choice of employment, to just and favorable conditions of work and to protection against unemployment.

(2) Everyone, without any discrimination, has the right to equal pay for equal work.

(3) Everyone who works has the right to just and favorable remuneration ensuring for himself and his family an existence worthy of human dignity, and supplemented, if necessary, by other means of social protection.

(4) Everyone has the right to form and to join trade unions for the protection of his interests.

Article 24.

Everyone has the right to rest and leisure, including reasonable limitation of working hours and periodic holidays with pay.

Article 25.

(1) Everyone has the right to a standard of living adequate for the health and well-being of himself and of his family, including food, clothing, housing and medical care and necessary social services, and the right to security in the event of unemployment, sickness, disability, widowhood, old age or other lack of livelihood in circumstances beyond his control.

(2) Motherhood and childhood are entitled to special care and assistance. All children, whether born in or out of wedlock, shall enjoy the same social protection.

Article 26.

(1) Everyone has the right to education. Education shall be free, at least in the elementary and fundamental stages. Elementary education shall be compulsory. Technical and professional education shall be made generally available and higher education shall be equally accessible to all on the basis of merit.

(2) Education shall be directed to the full development of the human personality and to the strengthening of respect for human rights and fundamental freedoms. It shall promote understanding, tolerance and friendship among all nations, racial or religious groups, and shall further the activities of the UN for the maintenance of peace.

(3) Parents have a prior right to choose the kind of education that shall be given to their children.

Article 27.

(1) Everyone has the right freely to participate in the cultural life of the community, to enjoy the arts and to share in scientific advancement and its benefits.

(2) Everyone has the right to the protection of the moral and material interests resulting from any scientific, literary or artistic production of which he is the author.

Article 28.

Everyone is entitled to a social and international order in which the rights and freedoms set forth in this Declaration can be fully realized.

Article 29.

(1) Everyone has duties to the community in which alone the free and full development of his personality is possible.

(2) In the exercise of his rights and freedoms, everyone shall be subject only to such limitations as are determined by law solely for the purpose of securing due recognition and respect for the rights and freedoms of others and of meeting the just requirements of morality, public order and the general welfare in a democratic society.

(3) These rights and freedoms may in no case be exercised contrary to the purposes and principles of the UN.

Article 30.

Nothing in this Declaration may be interpreted as implying for any State, group or person any right to engage in any activity or to perform any act aimed at the destruction of any of the rights and freedoms set forth herein.

End Note

*T*he thought to write a book on *human rights* had come in 2004 when I had an opportunity to work with a leading internationally reputed human rights organization, heading its Country Program as National Director.

I observed that the people working within human rights organizations and those who call themselves human rights defenders and activists were themselves unaware and exploitative of other human being's rights within their organization through a power hierarchy and structural set-up. I found their understanding of Human Rights to be full of ignorance. To my astonishment I found many of these activists mechanical and insensitive, unsympathetic and / or having negligible empathy towards other.

I was amazed and surprised – how can these people who are working to protect human rights of the world be so exploitative and violate human rights of individuals with corrupt rules, norms and processes within a human right organization.

If the system is so corrupt within a human rights organization how they can even talk of protecting human rights of people world over. But sadly they do!

I also noticed that many of the human rights defenders though might have read and undergone training; but during work they conducted themselves like machines as if they are heading a profit making exploitative market driven corporation.

Let me also add here that there are thousands of genuine, honest and straight forward human rights defenders and activists, who continue working on their mission to bring justice to victims without getting deterred by internal forces and weirdo characters working within Human Rights sector.

This example of Human Rights may be very similar if we extend the same analogy to other organizations and state that we may find an environmental organization indulging in activities of degrading environment, or a transparency organization is not being transparent to share their internal decision making processes, assumptions and methodologies to the world.

So that was the germ of thought that remained with me and after more than a decade when I had time and motivation, I sat down to understand and dissect the human rights declaration of UNHRD.

Through years my understanding on human rights has slightly improved on the factors and intricacies in the way the world of human rights functions – United Nations, International human rights organizations, States and government and big and small non-governmental organizations.

After years of experience I may humbly say that I feel equipped to pen down my thoughts on *"What is Human Right?"* with the hope that it will be a short, simple, quick and easy to book read for anyone associated or wanting to work with human rights.

I also realize that my thoughts and looking at Human Rights may be considered radical and I hope there will be sensitive, humane, caring and compassionate people who read this book – can, will and may understand my attempt to clarify concepts as a process of improving the overall understanding and changing the paradigm under which human rights framework is implemented world over.

Raj Doctor
2017

SHOW ME A HUMAN RIGHTS

DEFENDER, ACTIVIST AND

PRACTITIONER AND I WILL SHOW

YOU A HUMAN RIGHTS VIOLATOR

AND ABUSER

*T*ill UNHRD is not reformed and re-written, it will be extensively used and quoted, especially against the local state, government as a tool to put International pressure and catch media attention against abuse by the one who needs to protect and give justice to victims.

At least in that way UNHRD continues to be of some temporary good use for the society.

Raj Doctor